'Until one has loved an animal, a part of one's soul
remains unawakened.'
Anatole France

Herd Mentality
Leadership Lessons from Rescue Horses

Request for permission should be sent to:
Layla Rose Ranch
Annetta, Texas 76008

Printed in the United States of America
ISBN 978-0-9719731-7-6
Library of Congress 2024922050

Herd Mentality Leadership Lessons from Rescue Horses

By Matthew Hudson, PhD

To my wife who took me on this journey and introduced me to the world of leadership that existed since the dawn of horses.

To Cletus, Shelby, Layla, Buddy and all the rest of the rescues of Layla Rose Ranch for showing me what leadership looks like in their world.

Contents

Inspiration - Layla Rose Ranch Horse Rescue

Picture this: A herd of horses grazes peacefully in a pasture. Suddenly, a distant sound startles them. In an instant, every head snaps up, ears pricked forward. The lead mare, a seasoned paint, takes a few steps forward, her posture alert but calm. The rest of the herd, while tense, takes their cue from her. After a moment of assessment, she relaxes, and the herd follows suit, returning to their grazing.

Now, imagine a bustling open-plan office. A crisis erupts – a major client is threatening to pull their contract. Panic begins to ripple through the team. The leader strides in, her demeanor composed yet focused. She gathers her team, communicates calmly and decisively, and within moments, a plan begins to take shape. The tension in the office eases as employees see their leaders taking charge with confidence. The level of calm and confidence exhibited by the leader was infectious to the entire organization.

These two scenarios, while worlds apart, share a common thread – the power of leadership in guiding a group through uncertainty. When we think of "herd mentality," it often carries a negative connotation – mindless conformity, a loss of individual thought. But in the world of horses, and indeed in the realm of effective leadership, the herd mentality is anything but mindless. It's a sophisticated system of social organization, communication, and collective decision-making that has enabled horses to survive and thrive for millions of years.

In the pages that follow, we'll delve into how the dynamics of a horse herd can offer fresh insights into the challenges faced by today's business leaders. From the quiet authority of a lead "boss" mare to the protective vigilance of a stallion, from the collective wisdom of the herd to the nurturing (mentoring) of young foals, the equine world is rich with leadership lessons waiting to be discovered. At least that is what I have to come to learn from our Horse Rescue Layla Rose Ranch.

In an age of artificial intelligence, big data, and lightning-fast digital communication, you are probably asking what the heck horses can teach us about leading in the modern world? The truth is, five years ago, I would have asked that very same question. But in the Spring of 2020, everything changed.

My company, like all companies in the US, were ordered to shut down and go virtual. This meant that we all had to work from our homes instead of the office. I was the CXO of a retailer based in Fort Worth, Texas at the time. And it was my job to prepare the company to be remote - which I did admirably if I do say so myself. Everyone had everything they needed to work from home by the end of the first day. Everything, that is, except the emotional resolve to deal with a life of disconnect and isolation.

I, like most people reading this, had a very hard time with the "shelter in place" world of 2020. To maintain my sanity, each afternoon, my wife and I would go for a long walk just to be outside. My wife had moved us to the country just four months earlier, so our walks were not down sidewalk streets, but the tar and chip roads of the country. (Incidentally, for those of you who don't know what tar and chip is - think pavement on a budget.)

As we walked, we always passed the same pasture. And in this pasture were some horses - one in particular that my wife could not stop talking about. He was a proud gelding (male) horse about 4 years old. You could tell that he had had a hard life, and his temperament was one of "get off my pasture." He was always muddy and would turn his butt to my wife as she would yell, " hello handsome" as we would pass by.

As COVID time drug on, the walks went from once a day to twice a day and they always included that path to the horse. Over time, he would soften to my wife and eventually come running when she came by. Her love and kindness for him was refreshing to him and you could see it.

Each day, my wife would spend our walk times trying to convince me to buy that horse. And as all good husbands who eventually know they have no choice, I knocked on the door of the house next to that pasture and asked to buy him.

His name was Cletus, a champaign Tennessee Walker. And that was our first horse rescue. She moved him to a boarding stable a few miles away from our home and began the long journey with him to recover his heart. Today, my wife would tell you that Cletus is her "heart horse." The bond they have is something else. And yes, Cletus is the horse on the cover of this book.

The truth is that my wife has had a very difficult life. And is a big introvert. You could see the two of them connect over their life experiences. The impact he had on her was remarkable. She would say that Cletus rescued her. And when she said, "I found another horse we have to help", it didn't take as many "walks" before I said yes this time.

That was our first experience with horses. We did not grow up with them. And while I have a PhD in Organizational Behavior, I had a PhO when it came to horses. About a year later, my wife declared "we are not going fast enough. Rescuing one horse at a time is not going to work. We need to do more." So, we bought 11 acres - a football field and a half from our home - and built Layla Rose Ranch - a dedicated, 501(c)3 horse rescue.

We opened our rescue facility in the summer of 2022. And it is through watching my wife work with the horses, learning from her daily and observing the behavior of the horses that I came to see the amazing leadership lessons that exist for us humans from horses.

I am constantly amazed how well I can predict what the horse will do when we first rescue them and start their rebuilding process. Even my wife has commented on how impressed she is with my "quick study" The truth is, I simply apply "what people would do" in a situation to what the horse will do - and it is amazing how similar all the reactions are.

Horse Rescues are one of those endeavors that people love to hear about, but the truth is, like all non-profits, we are reliant on donations to be able to function. Which brings us to this book. I wrote this as a fundraiser for Layla Rose Ranch. 100% of the profits from the sales of this book will go to the care of a rescue horse to help them rebuild their lives and find a forever home. So even if you don't like this book, at least you helped save a horse from slaughter.

Leadership is timeless in its nature. Despite our technological advances, the core principles of effective leadership – clear communication, decisiveness, empathy, adaptability – remain as crucial now as they were when our ancestors first began to domesticate horses thousands of years ago.

Moreover, in our increasingly virtual and disconnected world, the horse herd reminds us of the profound importance of presence, of what non-verbal communication is saying, and of the power of a cohesive group working in harmony. I think these lessons are more relevant than ever in today's business landscape.

As we embark on this journey together, I invite you to open your mind to the wisdom of the herd. Whether you're a seasoned CEO, an entrepreneur, a manager, or an aspiring leader, the insights you'll gain from horses will provide you with a cool perspective on leadership – one that is both ancient and surprisingly applicable to the challenges we face in business today.

I will repeat myself sometimes along the way. The desire was to write a book that each chapter could stand on its own. So, if you are only interested in training, you can read the chapter on training and get some ideas and insight without having to read all the previous chapters.

So, let's saddle up (sorry) and begin our exploration of how understanding herd mentality can make you a more effective, intuitive, and inspiring leader.

Welcome to the herd.

Chapter 1: The Herd Mentality: Understanding Herd Leadership

When we think of traditional leadership in the business world, certain images often come to mind: the charismatic CEO delivering a rousing speech, the strict manager keeping tight control over their team, or perhaps the visionary entrepreneur charting a bold new course. While these archetypes have their place, the world of horses offers us a different, and often more nuanced, view of what effective leadership can (and probably should) look like.

In a horse herd, leadership is not about dominance or control. It's about earning trust, providing security, and guiding the group towards collective success. It is a world of learned behaviors - both good and bad - that shape the culture of the herd. I have had the privilege of interviewing and learning from many successful CEOs from companies of all sizes from $1M in annual revenues to $3B. And there are some pretty famous names you would recognize, but I will refrain from name-dropping to make me look cooler than I actually am.

All of these leaders told me one thing - the most important part of any company is the company culture. It is a living, breathing part of the organization. It determines the type of leaders you attract, develop and grow or decline with.

Culturrific! was my first book derived from my dissertation for my PhD. It is all about how a culture develops and makes or breaks a company or organization - whether it be for profit or non-profit. And while this book is not going to go deep into that topic, one thing we do know and must state from the wisdom of all of those CEOs I have interviewed through my career - the best leadership principles in the world - from people or horses - are only effective if the corporate culture allows it.

So, let that serve as our "disclaimer" on the leadership principles here. The truth is, when I was consulting with businesses, the majority of the time, the failure of the business could easily be tied to the culture. Core Values posters and Mission Statements on the wall or well fashioned strategy plans are no match for the company culture. As Peter Drucker says, "culture eats strategy for breakfast."

All that to say, you may need to examine your company culture as you work on these principles our horse friends are teaching us. Oftentimes, people will discard leadership advice because it fails, when in fact the advice is sound, the culture is not.

So, what do horses have to say about leadership? Let's start with the roles in the herd.

The Lead Mare: Quiet Authority

In most horse herds, the leader is not the strongest stallion, as you might assume, but often an experienced mare. We affectionately call her the "boss" mare. Even if the leader is a male, there is always a boss mare. At Layla Rose Ranch, our boss mare is Shelby. She was the second rescue we brought in, but the first female.

This lead (boss) mare doesn't rule through aggression or shows of strength. Instead, her leadership is characterized in four areas.

Confidence and Calmness
The boss mare exudes a quiet confidence that reassures the herd. In times of uncertainty, her calm demeanor prevents panic and promotes clear thinking. Even when she runs, it is a controlled gait and not panic that she leads with.

Clear Communication

Through subtle body language and vocalizations, the boss mare conveys her intentions and decisions to the herd effectively. It is amazing to see what she can get the herd to do by simply pinning her ears back.

Decisiveness

When action is needed, the boss mare doesn't hesitate. Her quick, assured decisions keep the herd safe and moving in the right direction. Horses can hear a sound from over two miles away. And when they do, they look to their leader to see if she thinks it is anything to worry about.

Protectiveness

While often not the physically strongest, the boss mare is constantly vigilant, always putting the welfare of the herd first. She is quick with instruction to move the herd to safety.

Translating these qualities to the business world can transform our approach to leadership. Imagine a CEO who leads not through intimidation or charisma alone, but through a calm, assured presence that inspires confidence in their team. This leader communicates clearly and consistently, makes decisions promptly when needed, and always prioritizes the well-being of their 'herd' — the employees and the company as a whole.

In my experience, I find that people think the best leaders are charismatic and gregarious. And truthfully, people do respond to a good speaker. But today's employees want to feel safe and secure as much as they want to feel inspired. You will notice that the boss mare isn't known for her great speeches or "overcoming" story in life. (well, maybe in a Disney movie, but not in our pastures.)

The Stallion: Strength in Service

While not typically the primary decision-maker, the stallion plays a crucial role in the herd. At our Rescue, we have no stallions, but some geldings - these are horses that used to be stallions but have been "gelded" or "neutered." Whether it is a stallion or gelding, there is always a lead male in the herd working with the lead mare. These horses have three specific responsibilities.

Protection
The stallion often positions himself at the rear or side of the herd, ready to defend against threats. He regularly eats with eyes up rather than down.

Motivation
During migration or in times of danger, the stallion may urge the herd forward, complementing the lead mare's guidance. With any group, it takes more than one person to get the team moving forward and functioning well together.

I love to watch when my wife is trying to get the horses to move from one pasture to another or from one paddock to another. Invariably, there is always the younger stubborn horse who wants to do its own thing and not follow the herd. Cletus, our lead male, will look at my wife and then go get the stubborn horse bent on doing their own thing and bring them to where my wife wants them. Cletus is used to delegation and while he knows he is the lead male on at the Rescue and even asserts himself that way when new rescues come in, he still submits to my wife's authority - and to Shelby (our boss mare.)

Mentorship
Stallions often play a role in teaching young colts appropriate behavior and herd etiquette. While they tend to be a little aggressive at this task, they see mentorship as a key part of their strength.

We see this constantly at the Rescue as a new horse comes in. During the first 30 days a horse is with us, it lives in our Quarantine Center. This is a separate section of the ranch that has its own water supply, feed, tack and shelter away from the herd. This is because my wife has a heart for the "hard" cases and so she rescues horses that are dealing with pneumonia or EPM or other illness or disease. This time in quarantine is designed to allow them to heal past a point of contagion to the other horses.

Cletus immediately checks to see what is coming in and assesses what needs to be done. It starts when the trailer rolls into the ranch. He speeds up to the fence and starts calling out even before we open the trailer doors to unload. But he does not always fulfill the need. As with any group, he tends to see the new ones coming in as their own herd and therefore focuses on the protection of his existing group. Oftentimes, he will not even let the young one come into the group.

When I see this, it reminds me of the "silos" I see when working with companies. How the sales department and operations departments are at odds with each other. Or the field is at war with corporate. These silos create unhealthy competition, and your company ends up in different herds instead of one. And each herd has its own leader and its own protector. The protector role (stallion) is to keep the distance and disconnection alive. Have you ever experienced that before?

Studying these roles, we can see parallels with leaders who use their strength and expertise not to dominate, but to support and elevate their teams. These might be the executives who "have their team's back," the managers who motivate their staff to push through challenges, or the experienced professionals who take time to mentor younger colleagues.

Leader Versus Manager

I think what's interesting about the roles of the two leaders of the herd is that they are both necessary. In other words, a strong herd needs both a boss mare and a stallion. In business terms, I am reminded of the often-discussed topic of leader versus manager.

Years ago, when I was traveling as a consultant and speaker, I would often be hired by companies to work with their managers or directors to help them develop a stronger skill set in their roles at the company.

I would put two flipcharts in the front of the room and write "Management" on top of one and "Leadership" on top of the other. We would have a healthy discussion trying to define each of those terms.

What I loved about this exercise is how consistent the feedback and discussions were between groups. I would be with a technology company one week and a retailer the next. I even did this with the church staffs and non-profits. So, to hear similar responses and stories from the diverse groups was equal parts fascinating and sobering.

First, we would get a working definition of each term. For Management, we used:

Management = Getting Things Done Through Others

This is a common definition used by many authors in several books. I honestly have lost track of who actually said it first, but it wasn't me. For Leadership, we used a definition created by Posner and Kouzes in their books on leadership:

Leadership = Getting Others To Want to do the Things That Need to Get Done.

After we got our working definitions, then we would list characteristics of each. I was always intrigued by the fact that the group in the seminar thought that my point would be overly simplified - Management bad. Leadership good. You could tell this by the answers they would give for traits of each.

Typically, the managers in the class would list negative traits about Management and positive traits about Leadership. But it was a setup! I was not trying to juxtapose one versus the other, I was trying to show how BOTH are good.

The idea I wanted everyone to leave with from those seminars was this -

*You can be a good manager without being a good leader, but you **cannot** be a good leader without being a good manager.*

Let that thought sink in for a moment. Management is not bad or evil. There are great traits and skill sets of managers. They do get things done. But the extreme cases are often what is used to define the management. For example, the command-and-control manager. I used to work for a VP in a company who had the philosophy "I'm not here to tell you what you are doing right, I am here to tell you what you are doing wrong!" He was successful, for sure, but he never grew talent out of his division. He got results, but the company did not grow exponentially from it.

I remember a district manager of a retailer I interviewed who had a particularly interesting view of management. I was consulting with this company on a turnaround. When I was in this position, I would always interview the top performers in the role and the bottom ones. This is how I got a handle on the culture. The top selling district was led by a guy named Terry. During our conversation, he showed me his "management motivation tool". It was a baseball bat with tick marks carved out on the barrel.

He told me that each mark represented a manager he had fired. He told me when he brought an underperforming manager into his office, he would lay the bat squarely in the middle of his desk to remind them he was the boss and what would happen if they did not perform.

Could you imagine working for either of these guys? Yet, they both achieved results because they knew how to "get things done through others." I learned to tap into the true good things they were doing and focus on that versus the extreme behavioral tactics they used - tactics that honestly are what leads people to think Manager Bad. Leader Good.

The point of all of this is that there are positive skills in management that any good leader must possess in order to achieve real success. We often think of leaders as inspirational personalities that give rousing speeches. But the truth is, a rousing, motivational speech from a boss that has no substantive manager skill set is not someone we want to follow. We may be attracted to charisma, but we stay for the trust and empathy.

So, in our herd, we use two horses to achieve this balance. But in the business world, it comes down to one - You!

The Herd: Collective Wisdom

Perhaps the most profound lesson from horse herds is the power of the collective - the team. While the boss mare and stallion play crucial roles, the entire herd contributes to decision-making and problem-solving.

Shared Vigilance

Each member of the herd stays alert for potential dangers, expanding the group's awareness far beyond what any individual could achieve. There is a sense of responsibility to the herd (team) that drives them beyond personal achievement.

When I was CXO at a retail company, we had a practice of sending all new hires to "experience" our stores before they started their training process. They spent their first day just watching and observing - no one was allowed to "train" them that first day. I gave them a guide with prompts to make sure they were experiencing all parts when in the store and gaining the experience we desired. When they came back, we did a debrief with the new recruit about their experience. This practice helped them connect the dots and understand the roles of the different people and departments in corporate in supporting those stores. It made a huge difference in our training and in our assimilation of the new person into our culture. It also showed them that their (the employee) experience was as important as the Customer's.

You cannot have a great Customer Experience without a great Employee Experience!

Later, I started sending my team into the stores for an annual experience day. No agenda, just watch, observe, talk with customers and employees about their experience with the company. I cannot tell you how many great ideas came out of this practice. We had someone who knew what we were trying to do spend time as an observer to what was really happening. The truth is, no matter how friendly or approachable I was as a CXO, I was an executive of the company, the second in command, and the feedback was always filtered and tempered. But with these employees on their experience days, it never was.

The point here is that everyone in the company as with every horse in the herd needs to know the mission and be vigilant towards it together. The good of the company like the good of the herd comes from this shared vigilance for excellence.

Collective Decision-Making

When faced with a choice, such as where to graze or which path to take, herd members often "vote" with their movements, leading to decisions that reflect the group's collective wisdom. This is fascinating to watch. They don't even need a whiteboard or a brainstorming session or a Slack. They can do it with ease.

Now, I am not saying that whiteboards are evil. In fact, if you are like me, you have one in your home as well as the office. But the key here is that the way the herd makes decisions is quick, but they do consult everyone. Oftentimes, I see cultures where there is a leader who maintains command and control over everything. They will tell you it is for efficiency. But employees will tell you it is for ego.

Many times, I see companies who are not involving others when making decisions because of the conflict. They do not want arguments or tension. They see this as destructive and bad for the culture. But read this clearly - tension is good, debate and discourse are necessary and if voices get emotional it's okay as long as the goal is to reach a solution or action that is *best for the company.*

Too many people argue and get heated because they want their way. While the boss mare or stallion may allow and welcome some pushback, they are quick to correct a horse who is voting "what they want" versus what is best for the herd. In the business world this means that we want tension. We invite it in. But the leader has to make sure that all voices are heard and no one is "shouted" down. The leader must maintain the healthy line of tension that is for the good of company versus for the good of self.

Mutual Care

Herd members groom each other, play together, and watch over each other's foals, creating a network of mutual support. Horses will not sleep unless another hose is there to watch over them. Most people observing would not know this because horses sleep with their eyes open. But unless they know they are protected, they will not sleep.

We see this when a rescue first comes in. We had a foal who was ripped from her mother early. Her mother was shipped to slaughter, but the filly, only four months old, was saved by my wife. The filly was terrified. She saw what happened to her mother. She saw the treatment of all the other horses in the herd as they were being sent away and written off. And she was understandably scared.

Since she was on her own without any of her herd, she would not sleep. She would just wander. So, my wife stalled her to put her in a smaller space. She picked one that allowed the foal to know she was safe on all sides. And then she slept - for a long time.

Not having her herd, she was not able to sleep. Her herd provided the support she needed. It is amazing to watch the "bromances" that pop up between geldings (males) at the Rescue. I am convinced it is born from this principle of mutual care.

In the business world, this translates to a leadership style that values and leverages the diverse skills, perspectives, and contributions of every team member. It's about creating an environment where everyone feels responsible for the group's success, where communication flows freely in all directions, and where mutual support is the norm.

By embracing these herd-inspired principles, we can redefine leadership as not just the actions of those at the top, but as a collective process that involves and empowers every member of the organization. This approach fosters resilience, adaptability, and a sense of shared purpose – qualities that are invaluable in navigating the complex and rapidly changing landscape of modern business.

The Structure of a Horse Herd

To fully appreciate the leadership lessons, we can glean from rescue horses, it's crucial to understand the structure of a typical horse herd. This structure, honed over millions of years of evolution, offers insights into effective organizational dynamics that we can apply to our business environments.

The Importance of Understanding and Respecting Roles

In a horse herd, each member understands its role and respects and supports the roles of others. This doesn't mean there's never any conflict - dominance behaviors and challenges to leadership do occur. However, the overall stability of the herd depends on this general acceptance of the social structure.

This understanding and respect for roles is equally crucial in a business setting. When each team member understands their responsibilities and how they fit into the larger organizational structure, it leads to a few positive things.

Improved Efficiency

Clear roles reduce confusion and overlap in responsibilities. Clear roles also help break down silos like we touched on a moment ago.

In seminars, I often ask people in the class or breakout session how much time they think is lost each workday due to a loss in productivity. I get answers anywhere from 20% - 80%. In this context I am asking to see if they see how large the problem is. We tend to focus on the wrong things in cultures these days.

Efficiency gets a bad rap. It gets overtaken by practices like TQM or ISO initiatives in the company. We forget that the biggest robber of efficiency is employees not knowing what's expected of them. We'll get into more detail on this topic in Chapter 6 when we talk about "Why horses (people) don't do what they are supposed to do." But for now, consider that you may not need a TQM program, but better-defined roles and expectations.

Better Communication

Understanding the organizational structure facilitates more effective information flow. Whenever I read the results of a cultural survey from a company, communication is always an area that gets a low score. I think this is because we rely too much on email and apps to do our communication. People don't really feel in the loop if they are reading a post written to everyone. They need personal communication.

When I was leading a large team and needed to make a change or roll out a new idea or process, I always had a 3-step approach. First, we held an in-person meeting (with all those possible) and then added the rest online. Everyone heard from me personally what was changing or what new process we were implementing. Second, I would detail the communication in an email to each person on the call. Yes, this was redundant, but repetition is the mother of learning. Third, I would make a personal phone call to each manager and cover the bullet points AGAIN. So, they heard the information three times.

Honestly, I think it is the third step that has the most impact. When one of my managers heard it directly from me, they felt like they were part of the process and not just getting "communication." And since it was step three in the approach, the phone call was much shorter, and any gray areas were quickly colored in for them.

Smoother Conflict Resolution

Clear roles provide a framework for resolving disputes and making decisions.

Earlier, I shared that tension is good as long as it is devoid of pride and ego. And that is very hard to do. (probably should have used all caps on VERY in that last sentence, that is how hard it is.) I think the biggest source of conflict is ambiguity.

Ambiguity in the workplace often stems from:

- Unclear expectations: When employees aren't sure what's expected of them, they may either underperform or step on each other's toes, leading to friction. We will cover this idea more in Chapter 6.
- Vague communication: Just as the boss mare's indecisive signals could confuse the herd, unclear messages from leadership (read that you) can leave employees guessing and potentially working at cross-purposes.
- Shifting priorities: If company goals or project directions change frequently without clear explanation, employees may feel lost and frustrated, leading to conflict as they try to navigate uncertain terrain.

We have all been on the company roller coaster of the "idea of the month." You know what I am talking about here. Each month there is a new direction coming down from on high. We are all focused on our TPS reports (see Office Space) one month and next month is something different.

Culturally, what happens here is that your employees start to divide themselves in three camps. One camp adopts your idea and puts it in practice. One camp does not and keeps doing it their way. And one camp, the third one, gives some effort to change - but not too much because they are waiting to see which camp wins. Why go through the effort of changing if the company is just going to do something else next month?

Stop for a moment and consider the gravity of that last paragraph. Essentially, at any given time in your company 2/3rds of your company are against you! Reality sucks doesn't it?

Ill-defined roles
When job responsibilities overlap or are poorly defined, employees may clash over who should handle specific tasks or decisions.

I see this a lot in larger companies. A department would hire someone for a specific project, but when it was done, the employee was kind of left behind and wondering what they should be doing. Amazingly, they still get a paycheck as long as they show up to their cubicle. But they were not contributing to the team anymore.

Inconsistent policies
If rules are applied inconsistently or seem to change arbitrarily, it can breed resentment and conflict among team members.

This I see when a manager favors one employee over another. Typically, in a sales organization, the top sales professional can get away with a lot of bad behavior - not entering his work in the CRM, lack of attention to detail, tardiness, etc. But since they have the best sales numbers, the manager looks the other way. So, it is not the policy that is inconsistent, but the manager in how she applies it to the team.

We got here by talking about ambiguity. By reducing ambiguity, leaders can create a more harmonious and productive work environment, where employees, like horses in a well-functioning herd, can focus on moving forward together rather than struggling with uncertainty and conflict. To remove ambiguity, take inspiration from the clarity and purpose seen in horse herds:

- Communicate with precision: Be clear and specific in your instructions and expectations, just as a lead horse's signals are unambiguous.
- Define roles clearly: Ensure each team member understands their role and how it fits into the bigger picture, much like how each horse in a herd knows its place. Remind them there are no small parts, only small actors.
- Maintain consistent policies: Establish clear guidelines and apply them fairly, providing stability similar to the consistent social structures in horse herds. Remove favoritism. Be consistent in your application of company policy.
- Address concerns promptly: Don't let confusion fester. Be approachable and willing to clarify issues quickly, much like how horses in a herd respond promptly to signs of distress from their peers. I think all of us have been part of many a meeting where we discussed issues, but nothing happened. We got it off our chests, but no one did anything about it. Well, until we do it all over again at the next meeting that is.

Okay, back to our list of benefits from understanding the roles of the herd.)Sorry I got off on a tangent there, but it was valuable, right?) What else can we gain from understanding the structure of the roles?

Enhanced Adaptability
Paradoxically, a clear structure can make an organization more adaptable. When roles are understood, it's easier to reorganize in response to new challenges.

This is a BIG deal in today's business world. We are victims of information overload.

There is a term - The Knowledge Doubling Curve - that was first used by Buckminster Fuller in 1982 in his book Critical Path. He had noticed that until 1900, human knowledge approximately doubled every century (that's 100 years for those of you who cannot remember that school subject). By 1945, it was doubling every 25 years, and by 1982, it was doubling every 12-13 months.

Today, it is **every 12 hours**! Let that sink in. Overnight, while you are sleeping, the amount of knowledge on the planet has doubled! Now let's sprinkle in some AI (artificial intelligence) and suddenly our machines are running everything. Sorry, I know that is a plot of a movie.

But why the stats? Because with this reality, companies have to reinvent themselves on a regular basis. So having a culture that accepts adaptability is important. What I do today may not be what I do tomorrow. And employees need to be made okay by their leaders in this reality.

Increased Job Satisfaction
When people understand their role and its importance, they're often more engaged and satisfied with their work.

The truth is that people draw the majority of their self-esteem from their jobs. We were not created this way; we just behave this way. If things are going poorly at work, then you feel down on yourself. People make a direct link between who they are and what they do.

I studied this intensely when in school. In my book, Cuturrific! I shared a story about this study. I wanted to test the presupposition that people draw the majority of their self-esteem from their job, so we visited a 2nd grade class of children one day to talk about "Career Day." If you do not have kids of your own or your children are all grown so that you cannot remember back that far, these 2nd graders are about eight years old.

Before we had any discussions, we told them we wanted to play a game. We premade five signs and tied strings to the top corners so the signs could be draped around the children's necks. On each of the signs was a job type.

We hung one card around each child's neck and asked them to line up in order of importance. Who did they think was the most important? This person should stand on the left and work their ranking to the right.

The signs read: Doctor, Teacher, Lawyer, Garbage Man, and Farmer

Here is what happened. The two children labeled Doctor and Lawyer started to argue and push a little as to who was most important. They each felt they were the most important and should be first. But the Teacher knew that he was not as important as the Doctor or Lawyer, but certainly more important than the others so they immediately took the third place in line without saying a word. The Farmer, knowing that people who wore ties or dressed up for work were more important, took her place fourth in line. The Teacher and the Farmer both stood quietly not saying a word. We looked for the Garbage Man, but he was not in line. Instead, the little boy with the label Garbage Man was sitting to the side quietly sobbing.

As a tear ran down his face, I asked him what was wrong. "Please, mister, I don't want to be the garbage man! I want to be important!"

If we were looking for proof that a person draws the majority of their self-esteem from his or her job, it was there in the teary eyes of that little boy. We conducted this experiment multiple times mixing up the signs. We tried other roles like nurse in place of doctor, factory worker in place of farmer and even expanded into third graders. Each time the results were the same. There were always two kids fighting over first, the middle children knew their place and the last place person was always upset. .

Where do we learn this? Television? Role models? Tik Tok? Parents? The answer is D - all the above. The impact all of this media or personal contact has on a child's life only gets stronger as we grow older.

The important part for you to remember is that

People draw the majority of their self-esteem from their job.

This means the more fulfilling your employees feel their role is in your company - the higher their job satisfaction - the higher their self-esteem. And we all know the connection between a high self-esteem and work. We have lived it.

Love that last part. It is powerful.

By incorporating these herd-inspired principles into your leadership approach, you can foster a culture of mutual respect, clear communication, and shared purpose. This approach not only enhances efficiency and job satisfaction but also builds resilience and adaptability – crucial qualities in today's rapidly changing business landscape.

As we close this chapter, it's important to note that like in a horse herd, roles in a business should not be overly rigid. The most effective organizations, like the most successful herds, allow for fluidity and adaptation based on changing circumstances and individual strengths. Sorry, I know that sounds like a disclaimer at the end of the chapter and I don't mean it to be that way. But I do want to be transparent about the fact that these are "principles" and ideas. They are not a recipe to follow step by step to get the results. You will read all, try some, adopt some.

Here are some questions to consider for incorporating these rescue horse inspired strategies into your leadership approach:

1. How can you cultivate a leadership style that balances quiet authority with clear communication, similar to Shelby, the boss mare?
2. In what ways can you better leverage the diverse strengths of your team members, much like how different horses contribute to the herd's success?
3. How might you improve the understanding and respect for different roles within your organization to enhance efficiency and reduce conflict?
4. What steps can you take to create a more adaptable organizational structure that can respond quickly to new challenges, like a horse herd adjusting to changing environments?
5. How can you foster a stronger sense of collective responsibility and mutual support among your team members, mirroring the interdependence seen in horse herds?

By reflecting on these questions and implementing some of the ideas from this chapter, you'll be well on your way to leading a more cohesive, adaptable, and successful organization.

Chapter 2: Building Your Leadership Corral: Core Principles

When you first step into a corral with a new horse, there's a palpable energy in the air. The horse is sizing you up, and you're doing the same. In those crucial first moments, you're not just meeting an animal; you're establishing the foundation of a relationship that will define your work together. This dance of boundaries, trust, and authenticity is at the heart of both horsemanship and leadership.

At Layla Rose Ranch, we are dealing with the neglected and abused horses - each with their own personality, quirks, and past experiences. Some are skittish, others bold. They have been mistreated and are wary of human contact. They often are overly pushy and lack respect for boundaries. Sound familiar? If you're a leader, you've probably encountered similar "personalities" in your team members.

In the horse training world, we call the basic foundational training "groundwork." This groundwork usually takes place in a round pen about 60' in diameter. The shape is intentional as horses move in circles. So, we are putting them in a shape that is natural to them and their behavior.

Every horse needs groundwork. Typically, you see a horse that is a performance or competitive horse do groundwork as part of its warmup routine. The methods used in this arena are varied and there are lots of opinions on the best way to train and do groundwork. But for my wife, she prefers methods that are based on building a relationship of trust between the horse and the trainer. She believes every horse wants a job and every horse was created for a person - they just have not found their person yet.

For many trainers, the basic foundation is command and control. With a whip and a lasso, we can get a horse to bend to our will and do as we say. However, the foundation of this method is fear. The horse responds because it is afraid of the consequences if it doesn't. I am always amazed how a horse flinches when it first comes in because of the memory of past abuse. Most horses we take it will not even allow a human touch. Consider this, a horse can feel the weight of the fly on its back. That little fly. So, if a person places their hand on the animal it definitely feels it.

So, my wife's process for training a horse starts way before the round pen. It starts in the paddock. When a new horse comes in, my wife often spends hours just sitting in the paddock with the horse. Our quarantine area, where the horses spend their first weeks with us until it passes a medical clearance, is an area with its own stalls, tack, water and feed supply. It is completely self-contained on the ranch to make sure that any disease a new rescue brings in is not transferred to the herd.

This small space makes it ideal for my wife's method. Rather than forcing the horse to obey her and allow it to touch her. She lets the horse approach her on its terms. This is accomplished by sitting with the horse for hours. Not making eye contact or forcing anything. Just being in their space. She often listens to her music and uses it as some quiet time for herself.

Eventually, the horse will become curious. It will start to drop its guard a bit and approach her. She never acknowledges it. She simply lets it approach and smell her hair or shirt. After a few times of this, she will offer her hand. Then eventually a touch. But this may be two weeks after it has arrived. The amount of time is up to the horse.

Why does my wife do it this way? Because she believes, rightfully, that if the bond or trust is established on the horse's terms, that when she moves it into the round pen to begin its groundwork training, it will respond out of mutual respect and not fear. And that since it is not based on fear, it will submit willingly. And she is right.

Now this is not saying that a horse immediately does everything she asks in the round pen. In fact, the normal stubbornness will appear at this time. She is beginning to shape behavior, and this means change for the horse. And who likes change?

So, the horse will fight to continue to do things its own way. But because of the bond of trust built by allowing the horse to respond to her, that stubbornness goes away fairly quickly each session.

Many years ago, I heard an equation of trust that went like this:

Trust = Compassion + Confidence

In essence, trust is not based on time. It is that moment when the person, horse, employee you are working with sees that you have compassion for them and confidence in what you are saying or doing.

Consider your own experiences. Have you placed your trust in someone quickly before? Of course, you have. Was it because they were older? Was it because they were the boss? (Wish that one worked.) Or was it because you felt the person truly cared about you and that they knew what they were talking about? You know it was the last one.

The same is true for horses. I have seen some of our volunteers jump in the round pen with a horse to "train" them and it fails miserably. They are very disappointed. They have watched my wife many times - even done some video training. But when they got in the round pen with the horse, the horse could immediately sense their lack of confidence in what they were doing. And they would not yield or trust the volunteer.

My wife is one of those people who make it look so easy that anyone could do it. But the trust equation is why the horse responds. Not her personality. The horse knows that she is confident in what she is doing, but it also senses her genuine compassion for them. Do your employees sense yours?

The leadership lesson here is that people development starts before the round pen. Before you ever start to build your corral, start with yourself. And before you ask the employees to join you in the round pen, make sure you have spent time with them, on their terms, building that relationship of trust. Otherwise, your training or mentorship is significantly impacted.

Establishing Boundaries and Trust: Lessons from the Round Pen

So now you know that in horse training, the first and most crucial exercises often take place in a round pen. This circular enclosure provides a controlled environment where the trainer and horse can begin to establish their relationship. The round pen is where boundaries are set, trust is built, and the foundations of communication are laid.

As a leader, your "round pen" might be your office, a meeting room, or even a virtual space in today's digital world. Regardless of the setting, the principles remain the same. Let's explore some key lessons from the round pen that apply to leadership. And as we discuss each lesson, I will try to give you a way to implement it as well.

Clear Communication is Key

In the round pen, my wife uses clear, consistent body language and vocal cues to communicate with the horse. There's no room for mixed signals or ambiguity. Similarly, as a leader, your communication must be crystal clear.

Develop a "leadership language" within your team. This could include specific phrases or gestures that have clear, agreed-upon meanings. For example, "Let's take this offline" could mean "This needs more discussion, but not in this meeting."

Warning here. Make sure everyone knows the language. Just because you know the phrase or acronym, doesn't mean your employees do. Spend time setting these ground rules with your team. Hold the team accountable for keeping them.

At Bridgewater Associates, the world's largest hedge fund, founder Ray Dalio implemented a system of "radical transparency." This included a shared vocabulary for giving feedback and discussing ideas. Terms like "drill down" (to explore a topic in depth) and "above the line/below the line" (to distinguish between high-level and detailed discussions) became part of the firm's common language, ensuring clear communication across all levels.

Respect Goes Both Ways
A good horse trainer knows that while they need to establish themselves as the leader, they must also show respect for the horse. Pushing too hard or being overly dominant can break trust. In leadership, the same principle applies.

Practice "reciprocal respect." When assigning tasks or giving feedback, explicitly ask for your team member's input or concerns. This shows that you value their perspective, even as you guide the direction.

Satya Nadella, upon becoming CEO of Microsoft in 2014, dramatically shifted the company's culture from one of internal competition to one of mutual respect and collaboration. He encouraged leaders to listen more and become "learn-it-alls" instead of "know-it-alls." This approach not only improved employee satisfaction but also contributed to Microsoft's significant market value growth under his leadership.

Another great example of this for me was a former CEO boss of mine. During our annual reviews, he always asked me for feedback on how *he* could do better. It was my review, but he wanted a review of himself with me. Talk about respect going both ways. He genuinely wanted to know how to improve. And this little action by him, had a huge impact on me and my leadership as I started practicing it with my direct reports as well. Didn't always like what they said about me but was grateful to discover some blind spots that I had.

Consistency Builds Trust
Horses thrive on consistency. They need to know that the same cue will mean the same thing every time. My wife uses the same visual cue for a behavior with every horse. Your team members are no different. Consistent behavior from you as a leader builds a sense of security and trust.

Create a "leadership consistency checklist." This could include things like "I will always start meetings on time," or "I will provide feedback within 48 hours of receiving a project." Share this with your team and hold yourself accountable.

Boundaries are Necessary for Safety and Growth
In the round pen, boundaries keep both horse and trainer safe. They also provide a framework within which the horse can learn and grow. Believe it or not, the horse actually wants to do well. They want to work. In your leadership corral, clear boundaries serve a similar purpose. Especially when you consider your employees are mostly the same way - they want to work, and they want to perform well.

Collaboratively create a "team charter" that outlines expectations, boundaries, and shared values. Revisit and refine this document regularly as your team evolves.

At Netflix, CEO Reed Hastings and his leadership team developed a famous 125-page culture deck that clearly outlined the company's values, expectations, and boundaries. This document, which emphasized concepts like "freedom and responsibility," provided a clear framework for decision-making and behavior within the organization. It was so impactful that Facebook's Sheryl Sandberg called it "the most important document ever to come out of Silicon Valley." She might have added the longest as well. As much as I admire what they did, I do think we live in a world where your mission and purpose have to be communicated in less than 144 characters.

Developing Your Authentic Leadership Presence

Just as every horse has its unique personality, every leader has their own authentic style. Trying to mimic someone else's leadership approach rarely works in the long run. Instead, focus on developing your authentic leadership presence.

Know Your Strengths and Weaknesses

A skilled horse trainer knows their own strengths and limitations. They play to their strengths and work on improving their weaknesses. For example, my wife is a master at the groundwork. But she is not as skilled when it comes to getting the horse under saddle. She will often bring in another person to help with that part. She wants the horse to have the same trust at all levels of its development. As a leader, self-awareness is equally crucial.

Conduct a personal SWOT (Strengths, Weaknesses, Opportunities, Threats) analysis of your leadership style. Share this with a trusted mentor or coach and create a development plan based on your insights.

Jack Welch, former CEO of General Electric, was known for his rigorous self-assessment and continuous learning. He regularly sought feedback from employees at all levels and was open about his own areas for improvement. This self-awareness allowed him to evolve his leadership style over his 20-year tenure, contributing to GE's remarkable growth during that period.

My favorite lesson from Jack Welch was the concept of MBWA - Management by Wandering Around. The idea was to regularly wander around the office or plant and observe. The key is in the term wandering. This means no planned events with the employees. They did not know he was coming. He didn't want it that way. He wanted raw, unfiltered content to enter his brain through his experiences.

Be Consistent, Even When It's Difficult

Horses can sense incongruence - quickly. If you're trying to project calm but are internally anxious, the horse will pick up on it. Even when you are on their back. It is amazing to see how a horse responds to a different rider. They know if the rider is tense or nervous. They can sense it, and it shows in its response to the rider's commands.

Your team members have a similar sixth sense. You may not realize it, but they do. Authenticity means being consistent in your words, actions, and emotions.

Start a "leadership congruence journal." At the end of each day, reflect on moments where your external actions aligned (or didn't align) with your internal state. Use these reflections to work on greater consistency.

During the COVID pandemic of 2020, I got a front row seat to watch my CEO handle the crisis with amazing calmness. None of us leaders had any clue what was going to happen, and he actually used that fact to fuel his optimism. He kept everyone on the team engaged and operating out of respect and not fear. Sound familiar?

We had to layoff employees and make cuts to survive. But not once did anyone ever lose the sense that this too shall pass and that life would return to normal. In fact, we took the time to plan for the new normal. For example, we knew we had to make payroll cuts, but rather than charge each department head with cutting 10%, we evaluated and stack-ranked our employees. Our approach was to layoff the bottom performers - regardless of what department they were in. While this approach allowed us to come back even stronger, it was scary to see a department cut deeply and another one have no cuts at all. But we followed a process, and it worked.

I share that last story because I don't believe we would have been successful if it was not for the calm leadership we had at that time. How can you be so strategic if everyone is panicking? You can't.

Adapt Your Style, Not Your Core

Different horses respond to different approaches, but a good trainer doesn't fundamentally change who they are for each horse. They adapt their techniques while staying true to their core principles. As a leader, you'll need to adjust your approach for different team members, but your fundamental values and leadership philosophy should remain consistent.

Create a "leadership philosophy statement" that outlines your core values and principles as a leader. Use this as a touchstone when you need to adapt your approach to different situations or team members.

Keep in mind, this is not to supplant the company's core values. These are for you as a leader to help guide you and ground you in your role as a people developer. Evidence has proven that if we write something down we are more likely to remember and do it.

Alan Mulally, former CEO of Ford Motor Company, brought his core leadership principles from Boeing when he joined Ford in 2006. His philosophy of transparent communication and accountability (embodied in his famous "data doesn't lie" approach) remained constant, but he adapted his style to fit Ford's culture and the challenges of the automotive industry. This adaptability, combined with consistency in core principles, was crucial in Ford's turnaround during his tenure.

Build Trust Through Vulnerability

In horse training, there are moments when you need to let your guard down and connect with the horse on an emotional level. A horse does not respond to the pressure placed on it in training. It actually responds to the release of the pressure. (More on that in Chapter 5) As you are training the horse (groundwork) you are applying pressure to make it move it a certain direction or in a certain manner. When you release that pressure and allow them to relax, that is when the horse connects with your idea.

The same is true in leadership. Showing appropriate vulnerability - you giving your employees your eyes - can deepen trust and respect.

Schedule regular "learning from failures" or "autopsies" (as I like to call them) sessions with your team. Start by sharing one of your own recent mistakes and what you learned from it. Encourage team members to do the same in a blame-free environment.

In 2015, Airbnb faced a crisis when it was revealed that some hosts were discriminating against guests based on race. CEO Brian Chesky responded with remarkable vulnerability, admitting that he and the company had been slow to address the issue. He openly shared his learning process, and the steps Airbnb was taking to combat discrimination. This vulnerable approach helped rebuild trust with both hosts and guests.

When faced with a challenging leadership situation, consider my wife - the compassionate horse trainer. She didn't use force or intimidation to work with horses. Instead, she has an uncanny ability to read a horse's body language, to understand what it was thinking and feeling, and to communicate in a way the horse could understand.

My wife's approach is all about patience, observation, and clear communication. She says, "First, you go with the horse. Then the horse goes with you. Then you go together." I'm not sure where she got that from, but this philosophy applies beautifully to leadership.

As leaders, we need to embody that same spirit. We need to first understand our team members - their motivations, fears, strengths, and weaknesses. Then, we can guide them in the direction we need to go. Finally, we can move forward together towards our shared goals.

When you're facing a difficult situation with a team member, ask yourself: "What would a horse trainer do?" (For me, I get to ask what would my wife do?) Would she push harder, or would she take a step back and try to see the situation from the horse's perspective? Would she raise her voice, or would he find a clearer, calmer way to communicate?

This approach is reminiscent of how Indra Nooyi led PepsiCo during her tenure as CEO. Known for her empathetic leadership style, Nooyi made it a point to understand the perspectives of employees at all levels. She famously wrote letters to the parents of her senior executives, thanking them for the gift of their child to PepsiCo. This deep understanding of her team members' backgrounds and motivations allowed her to lead more effectively, guiding PepsiCo through significant transformations in the food and beverage industry.

Building Your Leadership Corral: A Continuous Process

Creating a strong leadership corral isn't a one-time effort. It's an ongoing process that requires consistent attention and refinement. Just as a horse trainer continues to work with a horse long after the initial training, you'll need to continuously reinforce and develop your leadership principles.

In fact, there are not 85 levels that a horse must achieve in its development. The groundwork exercises I have been describing here are fairly simple. The most common one is called lunging. This is when the horse is asked to run around the edge of the round pen with the trainer standing in the center guiding with a rope tethered to the halter known as a lunge line.

Many trainers do this exercise in open arenas or simply in the pasture. It is the most effective way to get a horse's blood and brain flowing. You want the horse to be in its "thinking" side of its brain and not the "reactive" side. This is when true learning can occur.

The point here is that the lunging exercise is used with the horse consistently throughout its life. In other words, it is not about having a ton of variety as much as it is consistency. Here are some strategies to help you maintain and strengthen your leadership corral.

Regular Check-ins

Schedule regular one-on-one meetings with each team member. Use these sessions not just to discuss work, but to reinforce your leadership principles and get feedback on your leadership style.

I learned this practice years ago and have always made it a part of my process. I hold a weekly one-on-one with each of my reports. This ensures that they get my devoted attention each week. All of us are very busy and the fact that everyone knows they have this space carved out for them is comforting.

I never ask my employees to "wait" until the one-on-one. Direct access to their leader is important when needed. But the fact that we had this protected time made sure that we always stayed aligned.

Seek Feedback

Create safe channels for your team to provide feedback on your leadership. This could be through anonymous surveys, 360-degree reviews, or designated feedback sessions.

In my years, I have used formal instruments like 360 programs, online tools, and many more. After all these attempts with various tools, nothing seems to work better than a simple face to face conversation.

Now, if the trust is not there to start this conversation, then it is dead in the water. As an executive in the company or even when I owned my own retail company, I had a disadvantage - I am a "big boss mare." No matter how approachable I may think I am, my title always gets in the way. Before I ever ask an employee for feedback on me, I have to spend a ton of time with them creating and cultivating an environment of mutual respect and trust where they can freely express themselves with me.

And also note, that if you get feedback and take action on it, ALWAYS seek to protect the person who gave it to you. Never let the bus run over them in your expediency to take action or right a wrong. Your first responsibility is to the person who gave you the feedback. Protect them or you will never have any real feedback from any employee.

At Google, the "Googlegeist" survey is conducted annually to gather employee feedback on various aspects of the company, including leadership. The results are taken seriously, with action plans developed to address areas of concern. This commitment to seeking and acting on feedback has contributed to Google's reputation as a great place to work.

Continuous Learning

Just as horse trainers constantly learn new techniques, leaders should always be learning. Attend leadership workshops, read widely, and seek out mentors who can help you grow.

Over the years, I have been amazed at how people stop learning after school. Here are some sobering statistics when it comes to reading provided by a research study completed by <u>Above and Beyond Therapy</u> published in February 2024.

- 65% of Americans have not read a book in the last year
- 42% of college students never read another book after they graduate
- Only 32% of Americans even read for pleasure - less than 5% of these are non–fiction books.

What's my point? We stop learning. We rely on posts on social media for our information. Posts that are ripe with incorrect date or misinformation in them. If you do not have a routine of reading to feed your business mind, your chances of success are dramatically reduced. Sure, you can stay employed, but are you truly happy just being employed?

I get it. I hate reading. (Don't worry I am well aware of the irony of that statement by an author.) I have to discipline myself to read. And you should as well. It is vital - today more than ever.

Warren Buffett, despite his enormous success, is famous for his commitment to lifelong learning. He spends a significant portion of his day reading and attributes much of his success to this habit. His example has inspired many business leaders to prioritize continuous learning in their own careers. I think we can trust the advice of someone who has accumulated more wealth than all of us readers combined.

Practice Reflection

Set aside time each week to reflect on your leadership. What worked well? What could you have done differently? How did you embody your core principles?

For me, this is more monthly than weekly. I go out to the nature preserve not too far from my home. I take my journal and spend much of the day walking the miles and miles of trails and capturing my thoughts and ideas in the journal at various stops along the way. Sometimes I come back invigorated, sometimes deflated. But all times ready for the next month and better off for having done it.

Jeff Weiner, former CEO of LinkedIn, is a strong advocate for mindfulness and reflection in leadership. He regularly practices meditation and encourages his team to do the same. This practice of reflection has helped him navigate complex business challenges and maintain a clear vision for the company.

Lead by Example

Remember, your team is always watching. Model the behavior and attitudes you want to see in your team. After all, this is "programming" your culture. If you expect punctuality, be punctual. If you value open communication, be open in your own communication.

Horses do the same. It's fun to watch the horses gather near the round pen to watch another horse being worked in the round pen by my wife. You can see real expressions on their face when the horse fails to complete the behavior correctly. Cletus, the lead male, often "yells" at the horse when it's not performing well. Being my wife's favorite, he tends to get on the other horses when they do not listen to her.

The horses watching know good behavior when they see it. They also know patronizing or preferential treatment when they see it as well. In our chapter on Ethics, we will discuss this more. If horses can see it, how much easier is it for people? The sad truth is the number of leaders who think they are doing a great job of "hiding" it.

Yvon Chouinard, founder of Patagonia, is known for leading by example when it comes to environmental responsibility. His personal commitment to sustainability is reflected in every aspect of Patagonia's business, from its products to its corporate practices. This alignment between personal values and company actions has been key to Patagonia's success and reputation.

As you move forward, consider these five questions:

1. How can you make your expectations and boundaries clearer to your team?
2. In what ways can you adapt your leadership style to better suit each team member, while staying true to your core principles?
3. How might you create more opportunities for building trust with your team?
4. What steps can you take to become more self-aware and authentic in your leadership?
5. How can you encourage a culture of mutual respect and clear communication within your team?

By wrestling with these questions and implementing some of the ideas from this chapter, you'll be well on your way to building a strong, effective leadership corral. Like my wife, a skilled horse trainer, working with a responsive horse, you and your team will be equipped to navigate challenges, achieve your goals, and grow together.

Remember, leadership, like horsemanship, is a journey, not a destination. Keep refining your skills, stay true to your authentic self, and always be open to learning from both your successes and your mistakes. In doing so, you'll create a leadership corral where both you and your team can thrive.

Chapter 3: Culture: The Foundation of Leadership

Several years ago, I sat in the office of Howard Shultz of Starbucks. We were doing some research for a project for the Norman Vincent Peale Foundation, and I was a member of the team. All that to say, it was not my meeting, but I got to be there.

One of the questions the lead on the project asked Howard was "what is your biggest fear as a CEO?" His response, "being able to keep Starbucks' culture alive and well in the stores as we expand." His concern was that the more stores they added (and the faster they expanded), the harder it would be to preserve Starbucks' culture and unique coffee buying experience he had cultivated in the first stores.

In 2000, a few years after the interview, Howard stepped away as CEO and Starbucks started to lose its luster. Some say they expanded too fast. Others say it was because they entered into new and different products and got away from its core. Howard would say it was because of the dilution of the culture. The experience in the Starbucks stores opening at that time he was away was far different than the ones when he was CEO. The focus was on efficiency and operational excellence and not on Customer experience.

Howard came back in 2008 and dedicated his life to restoring the Starbucks brand by reviving its unique culture. He even chronicled his journey in a book Onward: How Starbucks Fought for Its Life Without Losing Its Soul. In 2017, Howard finally felt he had everything in place – specifically the right people on the bus – to be able to step down from CEO. But he spent 9 years grooming the right people and putting them in the right places before he did.

What is the definition of culture?

Here is where we go old school Boomer and dig out our friend the American Heritage Dictionary to help us. (Yes the actual book, not online.) There are multiple definitions of this word, as there are for all words in the dictionary. The interesting thing about each is how the latter ones grow from the former. See what I mean below.

Culture:
1. The behavior patterns, arts, beliefs, institutions, and all other products of human work and thought expressed in a particular community or period.
2. Intellectual and artistic activity and the works produced.
3. Development of the intellect through training or education.

NOTE: These definitions are for the word culture, not for the term corporate culture. Is there any difference? None whatsoever.

In definition 1, you replace the word community or period with company and Walla! In definition 2, the works produced (results) of a company. And in definition 3, read the intellectual capital of a company. I am especially fond of definition 3. It holds the key to corporate culture and more importantly to corporate culture change since it says through training.

The topic of corporate culture could be an entire book by itself. In fact, I did just that with my first book, Culturrific!. So, if you want a deep dive on how to design, develop and lead an experience culture in your organization, then I would humbly recommend that book. For this book, the brief description above is all you need to know. However, to effectively change or lead a culture, there is a little more you need to know.

John Parker Stewart, in his work Team of Champions, shares that "with a paycheck, you earn the hands and feet of the employee. But for them to perform, you must capture their hearts and their heads."

Truer words have never been spoken. How many times have you said to yourself after a poor performance, "My heart just wasn't in it?" If you are like everyone else in the world, way too many. This supports Stewart's and my point. You must have the hearts and heads of your employees if you ever expect them to take culture seriously.

With horses, we call this "getting their eyes." When my wife is lunging a horse in the round pen (this is making it run in circles around the perimeter and changing directions as she directs), eventually she will look at its butt and ask it to turn to face her and give her both eyes. To do this, the horse has to turn its entire body to face her.

When she has both eyes, she knows she has the horses' attention and respect. She also knows she is reaching the heart and head of the horse - think John Parker Stewart. When it only gives one eye, she has to keep applying pressure. A horse, like employees, will try and do the job halfway or not give it it's all.

It is a fact that a great percentage of your current employees come to work simply looking for the easiest route to a paycheck. These employees look to give the least amount of effort possible to get by. Truly this is their motto—"to get something for nothing."

A group of scientists were performing an experiment with mice. (I know this is a shock and hard to believe, but it's true.) They took a mouse and dropped him into a beaker full of water to see how he would react. The little mouse swam furiously trying to keep its head above the water so it could breathe. Eventually, the mouse's legs tired and he stopped struggling and simply sank to the bottom. The scientists pulled the mouse out of the water, dried him off and put him back in his cage.

The next day, they took the same mouse and placed him in the beaker of water again. This time the mouse swam, and he swam trying to keep his head above water, but not as long this time as he did yesterday before he finally gave up and sank to the bottom. It's now the third day – same mouse, same scientists, and the same beaker of water. They dropped the mouse into the water and guess what happened? The mouse sank straight to the bottom.

He had learned that there was no reason to go through the entire struggle and pain of trying to keep his head above water. In essence, the mouse had learned that if he would just sink to the bottom, they would take him out, dry him off and it would all be over. If it takes a mouse three days to learn he can get something for nothing, how long does it take people?

But that was a story about a mouse. What about horses, you say, isn't this book about lessons from rescue horses? Indeed, it is. And you can watch the exact same principle occur with horses. As a rescue, it is important that the horses go to the right barn or stall. We have to keep the herd separated for their health and safety. So, we want the horse to go to the same stall every time for feeding. Sure, there are eight identical stalls in our main barn, but we need to make sure the horse goes to "its" assigned stall each time.

This is important because new horses come and then they eventually go to their forever home which means there is a lot of turnover if we are doing our job correctly. We have some "permanent residents" who are rescues that we have felt it best to retire with us rather than adopt out to a forever home due to their health concerns.

Shelby, our boss mare, is one of those residents. With her suffering from DSLD, a ligament disease with no cure that will eventually turn fatal, we thought it would be best for us to keep her in our care for the few years she has remaining.

Shelby gets special supplements every feeding and therefore, if she is in the same stall each time, we reduce the risk of a volunteer giving her supplements and medicine to the wrong horse. So that is why the horses need to go to the right stall.

However, a horse just wants food, and it knows that all the stalls have food. Plus, for some reason, they always think the food in the other stall is soooo much better. (Another similarity to people wouldn't you say?) Therefore, the horse will try to go to the closest stall at first. We have to work to train which stall it is to use. And they will comply. It is fun to watch the barn door open, and the horses go to their correct stall. But this doesn't happen by chance. It happens through training.

It is very easy for a volunteer to enter the barn and say, "that's okay, you can stay in this stall." After all, it would be easier. But if they do not get the horse to move to the correct stall, then the horse becomes like the mouse in our story - they learn they can get what they want without having to do what we want.

Let's face it. You likely have a workforce with lots of hands-and-feet people who are looking to get something for nothing. In most cases, it's simply because no one has ever tried to touch their hearts and heads. They have spent their adult lives "getting by" looking for the path of least resistance. But what about yourself? Have you always been a go-getter? Or is there some point in your life when someone got to your heart and head that made the difference in who you are today? Is there someone who "got your eyes?"

Ron Hill was that for me among other leaders I have had - good and bad - that have shaped me to be the leader I am today. Take a couple of minutes to think about this point deeply. You could, in fact, be that person for the employees in your company.

A corporate culture is a living, breathing part of your company.

Until you accept this fact, you will never achieve greatness within your organization. Through my many years of interviewing CEOs from all sizes of business Fortune 500, Fortune 50 and even smaller market-sized businesses, the one thing all of them spoke about was the culture of the company.

But having an academic definition of corporate culture is not really of any value to you - you need to know how to shape the culture. And that is where the Culture Cycle comes in.

Exhibit 32 shows a snapshot of what this cycle looks like. Before we begin our journey through the cycle, there are two principles about this cycle theory that must be accepted before it will work.

1. This is a cycle. It repeats itself daily. These are no stages over time; rather, they are a daily routine that feeds your culture - either reinforcing it or modifying it. When a company or organization first starts, this cycle is more of a stage-development process. Later, it has a mature culture, which has already developed. If we want to change this "adult," the change follows the same cycle.

2. If this is a cycle, then it must follow the sequence outlined below. You cannot ride a horse until you have done your groundwork. And you cannot put on the saddle until you put on the blanket. These facts

about riding a horse are true for the culture cycle as well. There are no shortcuts in this process, so do not try.

The culture cycle states that a culture's programming determines its beliefs, and the beliefs determine its values. The values determine its attitudes, and the attitudes determine its emotions. The emotions then determine the culture's behaviors. As you can see, the cycle builds upon itself with each step.

You cannot have a set of values until you have determined the belief system. You cannot control attitudes until you understand the values of the culture. Let's deal with each part of the cycle individually.

Exhibit 32

The Culture Cycle

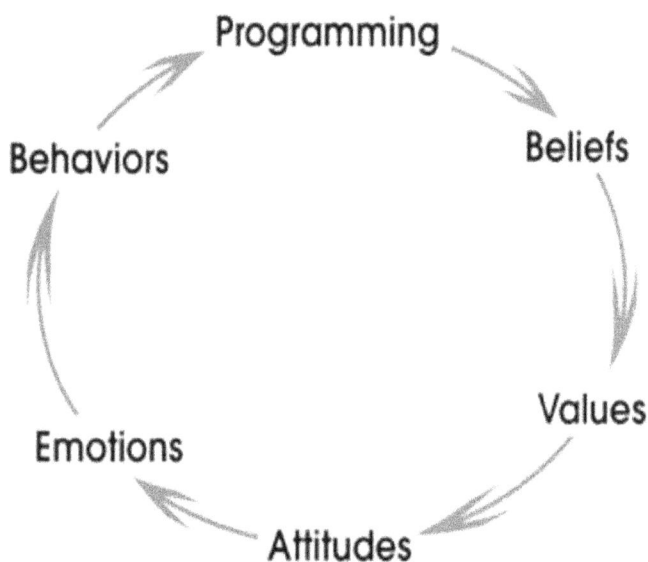

Programming

Behaviors

Beliefs

Emotions

Values

Attitudes

Programming

"Programming" is where the rubber meets the road. At first, this is a great asset, but when we have a mature culture, the parts of the cycle that follow after will filter all of the programming. This means that programming can be adjusted by what follows in the culture cycle.

What are some forms of programming? Well, first you must accept this:

Everything Speaks.

Everything we do, every sign we make, every decision we make on discipline, every process we establish, every meeting (you get the point) is part of the programming of the culture. Thinking back to your own life, you can see that what you have become is based on the guidance or programming you have been given growing up.

Have you heard the story of the teachers who were given three different classes to work with? The first teacher was told that her students were challenged and no matter how hard she tried, they would never learn at a regular pace. The second teacher was told that her students were average. She should challenge them a little bit, but not too hard since they would never be the smartest – after all they were average! The third teacher was told that her students were geniuses. She better challenge them like they had never been challenged before. And if they complain, don't let up on them. That's just what geniuses do.

After the semester, the students were tested and sure enough, the first class of kids – the "slow" ones – never made it as far as the other two. The second class of average students did, well, average. But the third class of students – the "geniuses" – did awesome. They blew everyone away. By now you have probably figured out that this was a setup. All of the students in each class were the same – average. But based on the programming the teachers had received; their expectations of the students were different. Their programming determined their beliefs about the kids and eventually their behavior showed it.

When the "challenged" kids said they didn't get it, the teacher behaved as if it wasn't the student's fault and in so doing programmed the students that they were not capable of achieving. But when the geniuses complained, their teacher wouldn't back down and her behavior programmed them that they could achieve.

My wife gets frustrated with people who say a horse is "too difficult to work with." She hears this a lot especially since she is pulling horses from auctions where they have been thrown away for being "too difficult." She gets a special joy out of rescuing these "no good" horses and proving everyone wrong. She discovers that the programming this horse has received came from the people who owned it.

Horses are incredibly sensitive to our human moods and emotions. If the trainer gets frustrated with the horse, the horse knows it. And when the trainer gets frustrated they start giving mixed signals and the horse is confused. But of course, it is the horse's fault, people say. But my wife often says that it's rarely a problem with the horse and really a problem with the people.

Beliefs

How we believe today is based on what we have been told or experienced or witnessed through programming in the past. If we have been taught that stealing is stealing and any form of it is bad and should be punished, then that is what we will come to believe. This whole culture cycle concept is easy to grasp because it relates so well to you as an individual in your life.

Perhaps you grew up in a different "culture" that felt stealing was only stealing if it was something we could go to jail for. Anything else is no big deal. So, we form a belief that will dictate the value we place on things.

Many corporate cultures have speeches about the importance of training or Customer experience, but do they really believe it? More importantly, does the culture really believe it? It's time for a sincerity check.

Your beliefs are the strong personal convictions of your culture. They are more than just ideas. They are grounded principles. Based on your past experiences within your company, when you introduce change, the belief might be "Just wait awhile, and it will all go away. He just read another Forbes article or attended another one of those seminars, that's all."

Keep in mind that with beliefs, you have to investigate what is really going on and not what is in writing. I spoke at the "100 Best Companies to Work For" conference years ago. I got to have lunch with Martin Brossman, the creator of the instrument and study that is used to determine the Top 100. He told me that the reason most companies will never make it to the Top 100 is the beliefs of their culture. His example was paternity leave. Many companies outside the Top 100 would look at what the Top 100 were doing and then try to imitate certain practices or benefits for employees. Paternity leave was one of the main ones that got emulated.

But it never took off. You see, the men in the company didn't "believe" (trust) that their jobs would be there when they got back even though the policy said they would. Plus, there was such a paranoia about being gone for too long that no one ever took advantage of the benefit. The culture's beliefs didn't support it, and therefore the employees saw no value in it.

Values

Your beliefs determine your values. What you believe about something determines how much value you will place on it. Here is where you start to develop Customer or employee experience value in your culture.

As you work your way through the cycle, we will see if you truly value Customers and employees. *If a belief is a strong personal conviction, then a value is the worth we place on that belief.* The stronger our conviction to the belief, the greater the value we will place on it. Therefore, the stronger a value it will be to your culture.

For now, let's go back to our stealing analogy. If you were programmed that stealing is stealing, then all of your possessions are valuable to you. You place great value (worth) on what you have – even if it's just a candy bar. You will have the same value on the candy bar that you have on your house. It is yours and should be respected.

We often hear the term "The Customer is always right!" If this is a true belief of your culture, then care and service of the Customer will be a value in your culture. But if you are like most companies, the Customer is king mentality is a slogan, not a belief. This plays out when one of your employees blows off a Customer because they are annoying them. No value here.

In a herd, you can see the value system come alive as they interact. Safety is one of the core values of a herd. You rarely see a horse sleeping unless there is another horse beside it watching out for danger. I think we would all agree that sleep is important, but for horses it has other meaning. Always having rested horses in the herd strengthens its security system. This is why they value sleep - not for the individual horse, but for the collective herd.

Attitudes

Your culture's value system will determine the attitudes that will develop as a result of an action in your company or organization. For example, in a company, if you believe time is a precious commodity and it is a value in the culture, then the employees' attitudes toward someone who is late to a meeting will be negative.

This late-to-a-meeting analogy is a great one because time management is certainly preached in most cultures, but it is often neither believed nor valued. I know this from the amount of time I have spent waiting in lobbies for the people I am consulting with.

I worked with a CEO who was fanatical about time. And because he was, the culture was as well. Meetings always started on time and in fact, you would often see people head to the conference room 10 minutes early so as not to be late. I myself would bring my laptop and finish my email in the conference room to make sure I was on time. I remember someone poking their head into the conference room one time where I was sitting by myself working on my laptop. They asked me if everything was okay and I said, sure, just working here white I wait for the meeting. "It's in 30 minutes," they said. I guess I got out of hand.

But what about the candy bar? If we were the "by the book" thinker, and someone walked by our desk and took our candy bar, what would our attitude be? If we were the "stealing is only wrong if it's something big like a car" thinker, what would our attitude be? It would be different, wouldn't it? The "by the book" person would certainly react based on his or her value and belief structure – negatively. They would "cop" an attitude and then get a cop. Oftentimes you can find this person going from trash can to trash can at each desk looking for evidence of a candy wrapper. Who needs CSI?

There are three basic attitudes that appear here: positive, negative and ambivalent. As they sound, the positive attitude will translate into a positive emotion in the next phase of the cycle. A negative attitude, then, will elicit a negative emotion. And finally, the ambivalent attitude is Switzerland – the country that is always neutral on all issues! An ambivalent attitude is unpredictable in the cycle, and in truth, can be more destructive because you do not know how to effectively program this person. Plus, the emotions that come as a result are unpredictable as well.

Emotions

The attitude that our mind develops then begins to translate into an emotional response or feeling. If we have been waiting for someone to start the meeting for 15 minutes, our attitude says, "This is wrong." Now, our emotions are starting to flare up and we're getting more perturbed by the minute.

Remember that CEO I told you about, one day he was four minutes late and at two-minute late mark, the people's emotions were of worry - was he okay? It's two minutes after; did he get in a car accident?

Emotions are tough because they cloud our judgment and exaggerate the situation – so much so that sometimes our behavior is irrational. The candy bar thief? Well, let's just hope that the person he or she has so ruthlessly violated never finds them! Meanwhile, the other people (the "only if it's a car" thinkers) cannot understand why someone would get so emotional over a stupid candy bar. They believe this person should obviously seek professional help.

We are an emotional society. We are not afraid to tell people how we feel about them and the horse they rode in on. It used to be that we held our tongue, but in the age of social media, we have become bolder and more aggressive with our opinions and therefore more emotional in our responses. We rarely take the time to think before we respond, especially when you only have 140 characters. (Although, I guess the masses revolted and they did expand it to 280. Which incidentally would fit the entire Gettysburg Address!)

Behavior

Finally, the cycle reaches its last stage, and we take action. The guy who was late to the meeting in our example gets strapped to the flipchart, his shirt and tie removed, and each person takes turns writing, "I will never be late again" in permanent marker on his chest. That's right, the behavior part of our cycle is when the cycle has made its first rotation, and we take action.

With so many parts preceding it, it's easy to see why the behavior in the culture is so revealing. How we behave or the actions we take outwardly are a direct result of the culture cycle inwardly.

So, what your organization's culture is today, in essence how the people perform for you, is based on a cycle started years ago when your company was born (started) and restarts every morning they report to work.

But the merit to the marker peoples' argument is proven in this cycle. Take our Loss Prevention people for example. Obviously, the programming they have received over time has taught them to believe that stealing is WRONG regardless of the dollar amount of the item. Therefore, they really value their candy bar. Their attitude is one of "you better not touch my candy bar" because if you do, they will get very emotional and probably see that you get five to ten upstate.

Probably the best example of a company's culture cycle at play is in the sales game. You hire a new hot shot that comes charging out of the gate and posts awesome numbers for the first few months. But then suddenly, their performance starts to lower and so do their numbers. Pretty soon they are producing at about the same level as everyone else on the team. Haven't we all tried to figure this one out before? You know the answer now. It's the culture cycle kicked in.

Immediately, when the new salesperson hit the ground, he was charged. His programming to this point had been "You the man!" and his behavior lived up to that expectation. But the programming of the culture started to kick in and eventually, day after day after day of everyone and everything around the new guy saying, "You can't sell here. This economy is dead. Our product is not as good as our competition." This programming becomes this man's belief. He starts to believe everything being said to him by the others. And their actions (more programming) supported everything they were saying because they were not selling like he was. Oh, sure they used to sell like him, and they would if they got transferred to another store or territory, but...

In just a few months, this fireball of a salesman was drug to the ground in a fizzle. His attitude changed to "no one is going to buy from me." His emotions changed, "I don't want to talk to them, they will just reject me." And his behavior changed, "Hey, has anyone seen the new guy? This is the third time he's been late this week!"

When I say that your culture is a living, breathing part of your company, I'm not kidding!

The Great Culture Mistake

The most common mistake organizations make today is that they are trying to change their culture without following the cycle. Here is a business example that really illustrates this idea well. Out of nowhere, Walmart came up to be the dominant player eclipsing the one-time leader K-Mart. In fact, today, Wal-Mart does over $1.6 billion in sales every day.

When the country started to notice Walmart's success, the leaders of other companies did what all great leaders do: they sent one of their people to find out how Walmart was doing it. Find the magic potion, bring it to me, and I will rule the world!

We are always looking for the next quick fix. This is why the majority of culture changes or reengineering efforts fail. We ignore the whole cycle and its impact. One of the things Sam Walton used to do when he visited the stores was to get the members to cheer. They would lead pep rallies just like in high school before the big homecoming game. ("For Walmart, every day is homecoming," said Sam.) One of the ways their culture celebrated and communicated this was through cheering. You could always tell where Sam Walton was in the store on his tour because the cheers would rise up from the members.

The "spies" saw this and took it back to their leader. "We have found the secret," they said. "We must get our people to cheer!" So, all across the country people started cheering. Pep rallies started rising up. And the companies were seeing some positive effect from these new initiatives.

It didn't take long, though, for these initiatives to lose their charm and impact. "Perhaps we need a new cheer?" thought the leaders. So, they toured the country again, hitting every location and every department all in the name of rallying the members to the great organization cause. And again, they had a slight effect on performance. But it still didn't last. Why? Because they were ignoring the cycle!

Horse trainers (not the good ones) fall into this trap all the time as well. My wife follows a method that has several steps in it as part of the groundwork of a horse. She could just jump to lunge the horse and skip the first steps like getting control of its hind quarters, but she knows that the behavior will not change if she tries to shortcut the process - in this example the cycle. The horse needs the foundation of the items that come before lunging in the cycle.

Exhibit Next

Programming

Beliefs

Values

Attitudes

Emotions

Behaviors

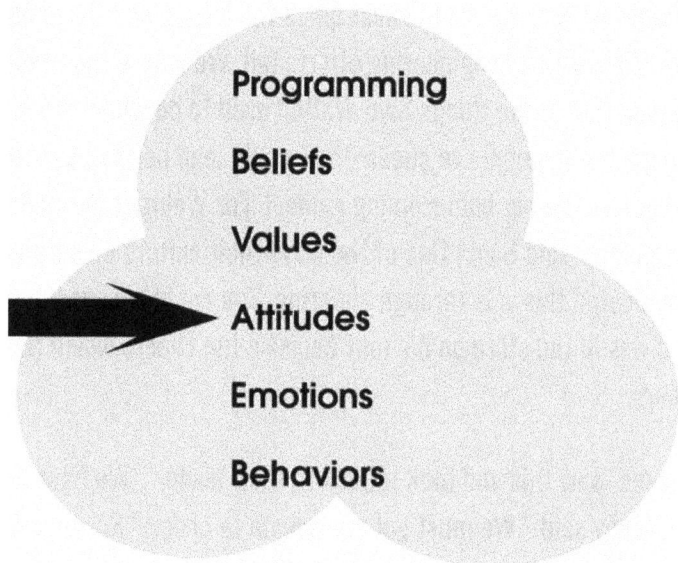

So many companies and organizations have fallen into this trap. They are trying to influence the attitudes of the organization, but they did so by addressing the middle of the cycle at the attitude part and tried to change the culture. The problem is that when the cycle starts to repeat itself, the beliefs and values of the culture kick back in and they change the attitudes back.

How many stories have we read about the online companies like Google and Zappos with their massage chairs and go-kart races at lunch? These are amazing employee experiences and part of their culture, but can you imagine sitting in a budget meeting with your CFO and explaining the expense for massages and go karts? These cultures were built from the ground up and designed with these ideas in place. Be careful not to copy someone's culture that is not relevant to yours.

Using the culture cycle, you cannot simply assign values and pass them out on a memo or email. You must follow the cycle. You have to first replace the old values of your culture, and to do that you must formulate new beliefs in your culture, and to do that you must change their programming. Obviously, the beliefs are the toughest part because it takes a while to convince someone you are serious.

The late guy to the meeting will still probably be late again if he "believes" they were just fooling. The company can pass a new policy under the guise of culture change that anyone late to a meeting will have to sing a karaoke song in front of the group. But if, in the past, being late was commonplace, then that is what the value of the culture is, and a new policy will have little impact...until they have sung a few times and find out you are serious. You see, every karaoke song is a form of programming the culture.

There is some debate among the horse community about how much horses learn by watching other horses. I stand firmly in the arena that says horses do learn by watching other horses. I know this because Cletus will often "yell" at a horse in the round pen with my wife when it is doing the behavior wrong. So even with horses, the culture of the herd can be programmed by behaviors.

Creating and maintaining a strong corporate culture is a complex but crucial aspect of leadership. As demonstrated by Howard Schultz's experience with Starbucks, culture is the lifeblood of an organization, influencing every aspect of its operations and success. The Culture Cycle, consisting of programming, beliefs, values, attitudes, emotions, and behaviors, provides a framework for understanding how culture develops and perpetuates within an organization.

Leaders must recognize that culture is a living, breathing entity that requires constant attention and nurturing. It's not enough to simply implement new policies or practices; true cultural change requires addressing each stage of the Culture Cycle. Starting with programming, leaders must consistently reinforce desired behaviors and attitudes, which in turn shape the beliefs and values of the organization.

The greatest mistake in culture development is attempting to change it without following the entire cycle. Quick fixes or copying practices from other successful companies without understanding the underlying cultural foundations often lead to failure. Instead, leaders should focus on building trust, demonstrating consistency, and embodying the values they wish to see in their organization.

Effective cultural leadership also involves recognizing the importance of emotions and attitudes in shaping behavior. By addressing these elements, leaders can create an environment where employees are not just compliant but truly engaged and committed to the organization's success.

Remember, like working with rescue horses, changing organizational culture requires patience, consistency, and a deep understanding of the individuals involved. It's a continuous process that demands ongoing attention and refinement from leadership at all levels.

I know that this chapter was more concept and theory than tips and ideas, but corporate culture is so important that we would be remiss if we did not include it. We didn't cover mission statements or go deep into the **Everything Speaks** concept. Nor did we discuss how many companies fail due to the misalignment between compensation and awards and the desired performance or behavior of the employees.

And let's not forget the hybrid working world we all operate in now and how it impacts the culture! The truth is that this topic is so thick and deep that it needs its own book. And there are plenty out there. I trust you are intrigued and will look to more resources for this topic.

As you move forward, consider these five questions to help you lead your culture well:

1. How can you effectively assess and measure the current culture within your organization?
2. What strategies can you implement to align your organization's stated values with the everyday behaviors and decision-making processes of your team members?
3. How might you create more opportunities for building trust and demonstrating consistency in your leadership approach?
4. How might you design and implement a comprehensive culture change initiative that addresses all aspects of your organization, from individual behaviors to systemic processes?
5. What methods can you use to ensure that your organization's culture remains adaptive and resilient in the face of changing market conditions and societal expectations?

By reflecting on these questions and applying the principles of the Culture Cycle, you can work towards creating a strong, positive organizational culture that supports your leadership goals and drives long-term success.

Chapter 4: Communication in the Herd

In the world of horses, communication is a matter of survival. A herd's ability to convey danger, establish hierarchy, and maintain social bonds without uttering a single word is nothing short of remarkable. I often see horses start to scramble in the paddock. No noise. No danger. Nothing happened that I saw until I noticed Shelby had her ears pinned and they all moved out of the way.

As leaders, we can learn invaluable lessons from Shelby and the other rescues about the art of effective communication. Drawing from our discussions on building a leadership corral and understanding organizational culture, let's explore how the wisdom of horses can enhance our communication skills.

The Power of Non-Verbal Communication

Horses are masters of body language. A flick of an ear, a swish of a tail, or a subtle shift in body position can convey more information than a thousand words. This acute sensitivity to non-verbal cues is a powerful reminder for leaders about the importance of aligning our internal state with our outward message.

There are 10 observations or "lessons" we can glean from the rescues on communication. Let's break down each and offer some ideas to help you improve your communication as a leader.

Align Your Internal State with Your Message

A horse's hide is very thick. After all, they can withstand a swift kick from one of the other horses without leaving a mark. We often have to tell a volunteer it's okay to give them a pop on the butt when they are not obeying. "But I don't want to hurt them, they always exclaim." "Don't worry you can't hit them hard enough with your hand to hurt."

On the other hand, though, a horse's hide is very sensitive. They can feel a fly land on their back. And when there is a rider on its back, the horse can sense every movement in the saddle. A great rider can move and turn a horse just from the position of their legs or their position in the saddle. No words. Just positioning.

Just as a horse can sense a rider's tension or confidence, your team members pick up on subtle signals you may not even realize you're sending. To communicate effectively, you must ensure your internal state aligns with the message you're trying to convey.

To help do this:
- Begin each day with a brief mindfulness practice to center yourself.
- Before important meetings, take a few deep breaths and visualize a successful outcome.
- Regularly check in with yourself. Are your body language and facial expressions aligned with your intended message?
- Seek feedback from trusted colleagues about your non-verbal cues during different situations.

Develop a Consistent Communication Style
Create a "leadership language" within your team. This could include specific phrases or gestures with clear, agreed-upon meanings. Consistently use these cues to build trust and understanding.

Horses thrive on consistency. They need to know that the same cue will mean the same thing every time. This is really hard in a rescue setting with volunteers. And the horses are smart enough to know they can play dumb with an inexperienced volunteer.

The volunteer can give them a signal to back out of the stall, but they will act like they do not know what the volunteer is asking. If the volunteer gives up, the horse wins. (See Chapters 3 & 6 on that.)

In order for the volunteer to be successful, they need to give the same signal for backing up that my wife does. A volunteer may give her version of the signal, but if it does not match my wife's, the horse will try to ignore it. But when it does match, the horse responds. This principle of consistency is equally vital in leadership communication.

One of the big issues we have in corporate America (and non-profit America as well) is the use of acronyms. We love our acronyms. And we overuse them all the time. How many conversations have you been in when someone uses an abbreviation or acronym and you honestly have no idea what they are referring to? It's happened to me a lot. And if I am honest, I have done it to other people as well.

It is not that acronyms are bad, it's when we use them as if everyone around us knows what we are talking about that is the issue. One time, I was working with a safety director of a company talking to them about PR footwear. We talked for five minutes and at no point did they try and let me know they were lost. How did I know? They asked me if there were shoes that would stop a nail from coming through the bottom to protect their workers from the random nails on the jobsite. PR stands for Puncture Resistance. It is a plate in the midsole of the boot that keeps ransom nails from coming through the bottom on the jobsite.

I have three middle school girls at the writing of this book. These ladies have a language all to themselves. I had to do my research and know that if I was "Ohio" I was bad, but if I was "Sigma" I was good. And don't ever be "delulu!" Anyone else have to deal with those words?

Try this:
- Develop a set of standard phrases for common situations (e.g., "Let's take this offline" for discussions that need more time).
- Create a team communication charter that outlines preferred methods of communication for different types of information.
- Regularly review and refine your communication practices with your team.
- Lead by example, consistently using the agreed-upon communication methods.

Practice Active Listening

Horses are incredibly attentive listeners. They not only hear sounds but also pick up on subtle changes in their environment. Their ears can hear songs from up to 2.5 miles away. In fact, they often get spooked by high winds because of the loud sound of the wind rushing through so many trees over that distance.

In leadership, active listening is a critical skill that's often overlooked. Just as a skilled horse trainer observes and responds to the horse's subtle cues, leaders should cultivate the ability to truly listen to their team members.

Here are some ideas for that:
- Implement a "no interruption" rule during team discussions to ensure everyone has a chance to speak.
- Practice reflective listening by paraphrasing what you've heard to confirm understanding.
- Use open-ended questions to encourage deeper sharing from team members.
- Create opportunities for anonymous feedback to hear concerns that might not be expressed openly.

Create Safe Spaces for Communication

At Layla Rose Ranch, my wife builds trust with rescue horses by sitting quietly in their space, allowing them to approach on their own terms. This patient, non-threatening approach eventually leads to a strong bond built on mutual respect and trust.

The horses we rescue are abused, neglected or sent off for slaughter. And that is a lot of baggage indeed to process and deal with. I have remarked to my wife how easy it is for us to see the baggage of a horse, but how hard it is for a leader to see the baggage of an employee.

You know this is true. As you read that last paragraph, an image of the person you hired who was fabulous in all the interviews turned out to be a completely different person once they started working for you. And you are left scratching your head and wondering how you missed it.

As a leader, you can apply this principle and check for baggage by creating environments where team members feel safe to express their ideas, concerns, and feedback.

Try these:
- Establish regular "open door" hours where team members can drop in to discuss any topic.
- Implement a "no blame" policy for reporting mistakes or concerns.
- Create cross-functional teams or projects to encourage communication across departments.
- Recognize and reward instances of open, honest communication, even when it's challenging.

Flex Your Communication Style

Different horses respond to different training approaches. While my wife uses the same principles in all her interactions with the horses, sometimes she has to adjust the style. For example, some horses respond to pressure from her presence. So, she uses her placement in the round pen to apply the necessary pressure to get the horse to complete the behavior.

With other horses, who are big on personal space and therefore respond negatively to that pressure, she will rely on a lunge line that allows her to send communication signals through the rope to the horse but maintain her distance while working.

Similarly, team members may have varying communication preferences. Some people are visual learners. They need to see it done before they can do it. Others are auditory learners, they can understand just by listening. Still others (most of us) need both.

Similarly, Customers have different communication approaches that they need. Some respond to email. Some respond to text. Some like in person meetings. Others like phones. Consider that you already know this and practice this with your Customers, but do you give the same courtesy to your employees when it comes to communication style?

Take the time to understand the communication preferences of your team members. Some may prefer direct, straightforward communication, while others might respond better to a more collaborative, discussion-based approach.

Here are some tips to help with your style:

- Conduct a communication style assessment for your team to understand individual preferences.
- Tailor your communication approach based on the individual and the situation.
- Encourage team members to express their communication preferences.
- Regularly seek feedback on your communication effectiveness with different team members.

Embrace Strategic Silence

In horse training, moments of silence are as important as active communication. These moments allow the horse to process information and respond. Outside the arena, we have a steel pole that is similar to a tetherball pole. It has a swivel on the top that allows my wife to chain the horse to the pole allowing it to walk around the pole but not leave.

This is called a "patience" pole. It is used after a training session to allow the horse to reflect on the session of groundwork or training it just completed. It helps the concept "sink in" for the horse. The separation from the herd and the inability to wander keeps it in contemplative silence.

In leadership, we sometimes feel the need to fill every silence, but this can be counterproductive. In sales negotiation, it is well known that whoever speaks first loses. Even in our dating lives, silence tends to pressure us to fill the void awkwardly. I know this is a hard one for me. I'm a yapper for sure.

Learn that silence is not evil. Learn to use silence strategically in your communication. After presenting important information or asking a question, allow time for your team to process and respond.

Here are some tips for the sound of silence:

- Practice the "10-second rule" after asking a question, giving others time to formulate thoughtful responses.
- Incorporate moments of reflection into team meetings.
- Use pauses strategically during presentations to emphasize key points.
- Create "quiet spaces" in the office where team members can go to think and process information.

Harness the Power of Emotional Intelligence

Horses are highly attuned to emotions. In our discussion of the Culture Cycle, we explored how emotions play a crucial role in shaping organizational culture. In communication, emotions can either enhance or hinder our message.

As we discussed the ideas so far, I can't help but be drawn to the concept of Emotional Intelligence. Often abbreviated as EQ (Emotional Quotient), it is defined as **the capacity to be aware of, control, and express one's emotions, and to handle interpersonal relationships judiciously and empathetically.**

Psychologists Peter Salovey and John Mayer, who coined the term, describe it as "the subset of social intelligence that involves the ability to monitor one's own and others' feelings and emotions, to discriminate among them and to use this information to guide one's thinking and actions."

I had the honor of working with Jennifer Shirkani back in the day. She is one of the country's leading experts in Emotional Intelligence (EQ) and has authored a few books on the topic that you should check out. My favorite is Ego vs EQ. She taught me that basically, EQ has five key components:

1. Self-awareness: The ability to recognize and understand your own emotions.
2. Self-regulation: The ability to manage and control your emotions.
3. Motivation: The drive to work for reasons that go beyond money or status.
4. Empathy: The ability to understand and share the feelings of others.
5. Social skills: The ability to manage relationships and build networks.

Her work with companies in developing hiring profiles has been eye-opening. By identifying the right candidate in the interview process through EQ assessments, companies have been able to reduce their turnover rates by as much as 60%.

She starts with identifying the ideal employee and building a profile. And then looking for people who fit that profile. Sounds simple enough. But in one example, the profile was suggesting the company hire someone completely different than what they had been focusing on for years. In fact, her profile suggested they stop looking within their own industry for new employees! They trusted her and she was right.

What does this have to do with this conversation? Well, you can have great nonverbal skills, a good posture, gestures, etc., but it is the understanding of how you are perceived by the rest of the world that is key.

Do you have one of those managers in your company (or maybe one of your friends) who likes to "tell it like it is" and uses no filter when they "speak the truth"? These people are damaging to a culture and to a team. And they justify their behavior with the "I'm just keeping it real" mantra. They have a very low

EQ. They are oblivious of how their behavior impacts others and oftentimes, they don't even care.

The art of communication goes far beyond words. As we've seen from our rescue horses, the ability to convey and interpret non-verbal signals is crucial for effective leadership. The ability to know how the world sees you is also important. I have been called out many times by my wife for what I said nonverbally. She knows me and knows from my posture and my facial expressions what I am thinking and knows when I need to dial it back.

She is teaching me to pay attention to my EQ. By honing your EQ skills, you can create clearer, more empathetic, and ultimately more successful communication within your organization.

Here are some EQ tips:
- Practice self-awareness by regularly reflecting on your emotional state and its impact on your communication.
- Develop empathy by actively trying to understand others' perspectives and emotions.
- Learn techniques for managing strong emotions in yourself and others during challenging conversations.
- Incorporate emotional check-ins at the start of team meetings to acknowledge and address the emotional climate.

Communicate with Authenticity
Horses possess an uncanny ability to sense and value authenticity in their interactions with humans and other animals. This innate sensitivity stems from their evolution as prey animals, which has honed their capacity to detect subtle cues and potential threats in their environment.

When interacting with humans, horses can quickly discern genuine intentions from feigned behavior, responding positively to those who approach them with honesty and clear communication. We see this with volunteers. They all are sincere, but because of the fear that some possess due to lack of experience with horses, the horse's "genuineness meter" goes off.

A rescue horse's preference for authenticity offers valuable lessons for leaders in various fields. By embracing transparency, consistency, and genuine emotion in their interactions, leaders can foster trust and build stronger connections with their teams. Just as horses respond best to handlers who are present and self-aware, employees and colleagues are more likely to engage with and follow leaders who demonstrate authenticity in their words and actions.

Moreover, the horse's ability to remain in the present moment and respond to immediate stimuli can remind leaders of the importance of being fully engaged and attentive in their interactions, rather than being distracted by past concerns or future anxieties. By emulating the horse's appreciation for authenticity, leaders can create more open, honest, and effective work environments that inspire trust, loyalty, and productivity among their team members.

Be genuine in your communication. Your words, actions, and intentions should align to create trust and respect with your team.

Here are some ideas for being authentic:
- Regularly reflect on your core values and ensure your communication aligns with them.
- Be willing to admit mistakes or lack of knowledge when appropriate.
- Share personal stories or experiences that relate to work situations to create genuine connections.
- Encourage and model vulnerability within your team to foster a culture of authenticity.

Master the Art of Timing

Horses are incredibly sensitive to timing. A cue given a split second too early or too late can confuse the horse and hinder learning. In leadership communication, timing can be equally crucial.

One of our daughters wants to be a barrel racer. These are the ladies who ride an obstacle course of barrels maneuvering around them at breakneck speeds. When you slow down the video, you can see how far off the saddle on the horse the rider is during a turn due to the G-forces at play.

It is amazing to watch these ladies compete. They can turn on a dime around all three barrels but still lose by .04 seconds. The key is in the timing for the turn. And that is equal parts art and science and a rider who can race barrels is incredibly skilled indeed. They must have impeccable timing when the stakes are so high with the difference between winning money and not is literally hundredths of seconds.

Learn to recognize the right moments for different types of communication. Sometimes, immediate feedback is necessary; other times, it's better to wait for a more appropriate moment. We will delve more into this in a later chapter.

For now, here are some tips for timing:
- Develop a sense of "kairos" - the right or opportune moment - in your communication.
- Create a communication calendar that outlines when and how different types of information should be shared.
- Be attuned to your team's emotional state and workload when deciding when to communicate important information.
- Practice the art of "just-in-time" communication, providing information when it's most relevant and actionable.

Master the Art of Storytelling

We are story-formed people. Even before we could write, we would tell stories. There is a term that best embodies the art of storytelling in our organizations and that term is folklore.

The term folklore got its name from the stories people used to tell around the campfires at night. The elders would gather the village together and tell of their history – their origin. Where did they come from? Why are they where they are today? What do they stand for? Who were the heroes of their people? It was the only way the information was passed on. There were no books or iPhones with multiple cameras recording in 4k and it was centuries before Al Gore invented the Internet.

Just like the stories of the elders, your company has its folklore as well - a whole world of stories waiting to be told to every employee and Customer. It is told every day in the break room, on a Zoom, in a Slack, at lunch, on the phone to Customers, in the interview to prospective employees and on and on. See if any of this sound familiar.

- "Be careful, Brayden did that one time, and it cost him his job!"
- "Our founder built this company working 16 hours a day; I think an hour of overtime won't kill you!"
- "You know when I was in your position; we didn't have computers."
- "You know when I was your age, we had to walk to school in 12 feet of snow!"
- "Well, that's just the way we have always done it around here."

What are your traditions? Don't know? Try some of the ones above. Is there an urgency addiction in your culture? This was Stephen Covey's idea in the book <u>7 Habits of Highly Effective People.</u> The term "urgency addicted" is for people who actually loved the overworked life. You know the type; they always eat lunch at their desk with a sandwich in one hand typing email with the other.

Does everyone complain all the time because they are always putting out fires? Is everything last minute? Who are the heroes of the workplace? Are they the ones with the highest sales or the ones with the best Customer experience? This one is tough because your executive's or manager's heroes and your hourly people's heroes are probably two very different people.

Do you want to know why people don't know who the heroes are in their company? Because it's not part of the process! It is never discussed in training. It is never discussed in meetings. There are no bi-monthly celebrations to brag on your people. As a matter of fact, in most companies, the tradition is to get together once a year for the obligatory Christmas party, and that's it. Then the employee has to endure a speech on how valuable he is to the company. Do you think they feel valuable if this is the case?

When I use the term folklore, I am describing a way to tell your company history and background that relates to the hearts and heads of your people - a way to "get their eyes". If you show PowerPoint or Google slides or the 80′ x 100′ color, glossy portrait of the founder to everyone as part of their indoctrination into your company, you are asking them to give you their hands and feet. You must reach them – relate to them! Tell them stories! Stories like your grandparents did, or the elders did in early civilizations.

Instead of saying, "The Grandiose Company was founded in 1943 by Ben There. He got the idea from people watching at the fair."

Try this story version instead.

"It's July 17, 1943, and Ben There is standing on the stairwell overlooking the midway at the county fair in Everett, Texas. He had been noticing the way people were continually fanning themselves with their tickets while they waited in line. And then suddenly it hits him. What if you could make a fan that was small enough to fit in the palm of your hand? A woman could carry it in her purse, and it would be battery operated. Excitedly, Ben ran back to the office and started drawing up the plans for the Personal Hand Fan, our first ever product at Grandiose. And that tradition of the invention is what drives us still today."

Notice the difference. It was like you were hearing a story about someone instead of hearing a lecture. And it will stick in your mind. Do you know the other reason people loved to sit around the fire and listen to folklore? It made them feel like they were part of something. Everyone wants to feel like they are part of something.

Horses are no different. Being part of something is exactly why horses are herd animals. A horse alone may look pretty on a hill, but loneliness will literally shorten its life. Horses are meant to be in a herd. It is how they were formed and created. And people are no different. They want to belong to something as well. Something that has purpose and meaning.

How do you tell your employees about your traditions or your folklore? What stories do you share? We live in the Tik Tok/ Insta generation, and they need to be entertained. Walt Disney once said, "I would much rather entertain someone in hopes of training them than to train someone in hopes of entertaining them." Walt had the right formula and so can you.

What traditions do you want to be present in your culture? Celebration? Recognition? Integrity? Care? Passion? Teamwork? Risk? Are your people afraid to step out and take a chance? If so, it's an example of the tradition in your company. And the traditions are carried from one department to the next from one employee to the net from one generation to the next through stories – through folklore.

Communication is at the heart of effective leadership. By learning from rescue horses, we can enhance our ability to communicate clearly, consistently, and empathetically. Non-verbal cues, consistency, active listening, trust-building, adaptability, strategic use of silence, emotional intelligence, authenticity, and timing are all critical components of effective communication.

These lessons from horses remind us that communication is not just about words, but about creating genuine connections, understanding, and trust. By mastering these elements, we can create stronger relationships with our team members, foster a positive organizational culture, and lead more effectively.

Here are five questions to consider about your communication style:

1. How can you become more aware of your non-verbal communication cues and ensure they align with your intended message?
2. In what ways can you create a more consistent "leadership language" within your team to enhance understanding and trust?
3. How might you create more opportunities for active listening and gathering feedback from all levels of your organization?
4. What strategies can you implement to adapt your communication style to different team members while maintaining your authenticity as a leader?
5. How can you better incorporate emotional intelligence (EQ) into your communication approach to create stronger connections with your team?

By reflecting on these questions and applying the lessons from rescue horses, you can significantly enhance your communication skills and, in turn, your effectiveness as a leader. Remember, like working with horses, improving your communication is an ongoing process that requires patience, practice, and a willingness to continuously learn and adapt.

Chapter 5: The Art of Training: Lessons from Horse Trainers

I spent many years training and speaking at conferences and companies all over the world. I was fortunate to have a terrific mentor early in my career named Ron Hill. Ron was a former instructor at the Naval academy. He taught me so much about training and people development and I am forever grateful to his mentorship in my life.

Fast forward a bit, as I was studying for my PhD, I got even more insight into the principles of learning. But nothing compares to the 1,000s of hours of training I have conducted through the years. What I learned is that with all the mentoring and classical study I had had in my life, it was through watching the way people responded (or did not respond) to my training that made the light go on inside me.

So, some might say I am a bit of an expert when it comes to training people. But here is what I have found to be the most fascinating part of the horse rescue - watching my wife train. I have been able to give her advice on what to do with a horse by watching the horse's behavior or reaction to her. Not because I know so much about training horses, because I don't. But because I would simply apply the same logic I would if it was a person I was observing. And it is amazing how similar horses and humans are when it comes to behavior and training.

Horses, like employees, want to perform well. Yes, some are lazy. Yes, some want to be the boss over you. Yes, some want to do as little as possible to get out of the arena. Yes, some cause havoc within the herd by pushing back on your training while everyone is watching. Does any of that sound familiar? Any employees you have working for you that behave like this?

Since you answered that last question, YES! You are now understanding the connection. My wife is way smarter than me when it comes to horses and their needs. But when it comes to training, I can keep up with her.

But before we go any further, we must first establish the purpose and goal of training. We want our employees to learn, right? But how do we know they have learned? We do not use a test; we look for something more.

Learning = a Change in Behavior

In order to be successful, you must adopt this definition of learning. We are not putting people in training to transfer knowledge for a short period. We want them to change what they do permanently - for the better.

Typically, we rely on teaching when it comes to learning. But the problem with teaching (no offense) is that it tends to be temporary. Not a long-lasting change.

Remember, we can do anything for a short period of time. Reality TV has taught us that. For 60 days, we can endure an island with little food, little sleep and annoying people who have no soap or toothbrushes.

So, your employees can watch a video online and pass a test. But the true measure of learning is to see change. Not for a few weeks, but for their career with you. We will go deeper into this idea in the next chapter as we open a can of "why employees don't do what they are supposed to" but for now, let's keep our focus and attention on training your employees.

In one of the workshops, I used to teach that focused on training I would start with two flip charts at the front of the room. At the top of one I would write TEACHING and on the top of the other I would write TRAINING. I would lead a discussion with the group applying pressure and then releasing it (more on that in a bit) to get a working definition for each. Here was teaching:

Teaching = Passing on Knowledge

The purpose of teaching is to get the notes of the teacher transferred to the notes of the student. In other words, get my notes (teacher) to your notes (student.) When this has been accomplished, then teaching has done its job. This is a fairly straightforward definition, but it is accurate in its purest form.

We give the lectures, and they take the notes. We give them a test. They pass it. We give them an 8.5" x 11" color glossy certificate to hang up on the wall. At the completion of this cycle, everyone has been taught, and we can expect all of the problems to go away and the performances to improve. Right?

The problem is that people use the terms teaching and training interchangeably all the time. But they are two VERY different things. While teaching is defined as passing on knowledge, the definition of training takes it one step further.

Training = Passing on Performance

Trainers focus on the "why" as well as the "how." They want to make sure the student understands the whole picture, not just their small part of it. Trainers also look for creative and innovative ways to involve the students that do not involve PowerPoint or Google slides! Remember, when the lights go down in the room, they also go down in the minds of your student.

Trainers want to know the student can do it, not just know how to do it.

Training is the key, not just teaching. And learning - a change in behavior - is our goal. After all, your overall objective is to "program" new behavior into your culture. You have established the values and beliefs of your culture, and through your learning about the culture cycle, we know that repetition is vital to programming your desired culture.

In order to be effective and achieve true learning, there are six focus areas of training for horses (and people). They are:

1. Prepare the Learner
2. Set the Stage
3. Establish Authority
4. Press and Release
5. Reward Performance
6. Repeat

1. Prepare the Learner

One of the most important things I learned from Ron Hill was that the preparation of myself made all the difference in the outcome or success of the training session. It took me almost a year to figure this out. Ron's style was to let me discover it. But I hated that style. Not because his approach ultimately shaped me into being a great trainer, but because I am so impatient.

I remember working so hard to be a great trainer. I practiced my presentations. I would do them in the mirror. I would record and watch it back to rehearse. Every gesture, every posture, every change in my cadence and tone was intentional. And on paper, I was the most awesome trainer who ever existed. At least that is how I saw it.

However, when Ron would train, people said he "walked on water" he was so good. And it made me crazy. I wanted to be that good. That is why I worked so hard to get there. But when I finished one of my training sessions, people would say "he did a really good job." But when Ron finished his session people raved that Ron was the most awesome trainer ever!

For one Summer, we were both doing the same training seminar, but in different parts of the country for our company. We would talk at night and debrief how our respective days went. One night, when I called to check in with Ron, I asked, "what are you up to?" To which he replied, "well, I'm just sitting here drying off my feet." That bothered me soooo much, I cannot tell you. He knew how to push my buttons for sure. I wanted to be as good as he was. I spent hours trying to hone my skills to do so. But they kept saying how Ron changed their life and how they really "liked" me. Ron even told me I was the best technical (meaning skilled) trainer he had ever seen.

So, did you ever figure it out you are asking? Thankfully yes. Ron let me squirm for months before showing me the light. Honestly, he had hoped I would arrive at my enlightenment on my own. And that would have been better. But when I got it, it was truly the most humbling thing ever in my career.

"Matt, he said, when you do a training seminar, you are focused on you. How am I doing? Do the students like me? Do they think I am awesome?" "When I am doing a session, Ron said, I am focused on them - the people in the room. I don't care what they think about me, I care what they think about themselves. And if my training will help them be better, then that focus is what will get them to realize *their* potential and become the best version of themselves."

Ouch. He was right. I was all "look at me!" Aren't I great? Aren't you lucky to have me as your trainer? So arrogant. So prideful. So much ego. And the people in my seminars paid for it.

I see so many people step into the round pen with a horse with that same attitude. They think they know what to do. They think they are human, and humans are mightier than horses - especially mentally. They get frustrated when the horse does not respond to their training. And, of course, it is the horse's fault.

We took in a horse one time that the owner was dumping. This horse has too much attitude and is not trainable, they told my wife. (My wife doesn't show much emotion, but I could see it in her eyes how wrong she knew they were.) Long story short, that untrainable horse is now living in a new forever home training to be a barrel racer. My wife turned that mare into a sweet, loving, submissive Anglo Arabian beauty.

She has done this many times, but it starts with her belief in the horse and not her belief in her training. She is very humble. And I have to work on her confidence a lot. We are very opposite in that way. I have to work on her confidence, and she has to work on my humbleness.

Focus on the people in the room, not on your content or your delivery. People want to learn just like the horses at our rescue. But they will only learn if they know you care about them. And not just your "agenda."

Preparing yourself is important, but we also have to prepare the learner. Being a rescue, most horses that come in are terrified of humans. They have scarred pasts of abuse or neglect. So, before my wife ever starts the process of training, she first has to *prepare* the horse to learn.

She does this by spending time with them on their terms. She doesn't force them. She wants the horse to know that she cares about them and will meet them on their terms. If you ever follow any of her social media posts, you will often see her just sitting on the ground next to a new rescue. No pressure. Not trying to touch the horse. Just being in its space.

Eventually, the horse will become curious and come to her. She continues to look away and act as if she is not interested. She allows them to smell her clothes and hair. She waits for them to engage. This process I am describing sounds simple, but sometimes it may be a full week before the horse even approaches her.

As the relationship grows, my wife will reach for a touch. Just one. And then be done. What patience she has. But through her method, the horse will begin to respond. And what was a "wild" unhandled horse will soon show up on Tik Tok with a halter and lead rope.

My point here is that if you have a new hire, don't just throw them into onboarding. Make sure they get to know their boss before the training. I see too many companies thrust employees into onboarding curriculums - that are important and necessary - but before they establish a relationship with their leader.

My wife is going to be the leader of the horse. She is going to train it and ask it to do so much more. But she focuses on the relationship first. Imagine a new employee spending the first week training and the only "relationship" they have is with HR because that is who is assigned their onboarding.

It is even worse with our video worlds. Much of the training is done online with videos. Are videos what you want your employee to connect too? Or their leader? I am not saying that videos or online learning is bad. They are not bad. I am saying that if you do not start with building the relationship between the employee and their leader first, you are skipping the most important step in the process.

My wife could force the horse to do her will. She can get a rope and a whip and force it into submission. But she knows that for the rest of that animal's life, it will do what is asked out of fear. She chooses the harder path. The path that leads to the horse responding out of respect. The horse knows it can trust my wife. So, it wants to perform for her.

How many of your employees, especially new hires, are responding to their leaders out of respect? If you are like too many managers these days, they respond out of fear. This is my boss so I better do what he or she says or else I will get punished or lose my job. That is their response.

If turnover is the number one expense to a company, is there any better investment than in the relationship between a new hire and his leader? Make sure the leader is going to the employee and establishing the relationship the way my wife does with the rescues before you start their training. You will see a significant difference indeed.

2. Set the Stage

One of the principles of learning taught to me by Ron Hill is the Principle of Readiness which says people will learn more if they are ready to learn. Yes everything we just talked about in that last section has to do with readiness. But now we are in the training session - in the room - so this is another type of readiness.

When a horse enters the round pen to begin its groundwork, the trainer starts by getting control of its hind quarters. This is an exercise of getting the horse to bend around its rear with its head facing the trainer.

Why do we do this? Because horses have two sides to their brains, the thinking side and the reactive side. When they first enter into the round pen or arena, they are on alert. Which means they are in the reactive side of their brain. But we need them to be in the thinking side of the brain in order for the training to stick.

So, this warmup is used to get them going. For people, when we enter a room for training, our minds are not ready for learning. We are still thinking about the conversation we had in the hall on the way there or scrolling on our devices as we find our seat. An effective trainer must set the stage for the training and get the learner "ready" to learn.

Probably not a good idea to get your employees up and have them turn circles to yield their hind quarters, but NEVER start the learning until they are ready. Try telling a story related to what you are training. Don't start with "welcome to the training." Start with a story.

Just like a schmancy dinner when you have a palette cleanser in between courses, you need to give your student's brains a palette cleanser as well. Your first task is to get them in the room. Remember their heads are still focused on whatever was just happening before they came into the room. And too often these days, it is a crisis or fire that needs putting out. Hard to listen until their mind is off that and in the room with you.

3. Establish Authority

When a new volunteer comes in, Layla, our four-year-old palomino mare, immediately sees someone she can boss. Horses will always test and see if you know what you are doing and if not, they want to be your boss.

Layla will pin her ears at the new volunteer. This is her first test. Then if the volunteer doesn't respond, she will close space, meaning she will get close to you. If again, the volunteer doesn't know what they are doing and tells her to back up, but has no authority with her, Layla will continue in and try to nip her. If the volunteer yells at her and tells her to back up, but again has not established authority, Layla will turn her butt to kick. This is the process a horse will go through to establish *its* authority.

One of the training sessions my wife will do with a new volunteer is how to back a horse out of your space. She shows them the signs like pinning their ears and what to do about it. (We will talk more about pinning ears in a bit.) What the volunteer was doing wrong is not demonstrating knowledge and establishing authority with that knowledge.

One day, Layla had a volunteer pinned in the corner of the paddock. She had her ears pinned and was moving in. My wife saw it and immediately went over and showed the volunteer what to do. You could see it all over Layla's face. She was so mad at my wife for showing the volunteer what to do. Evidently, this had been going on for a week and nothing was said about it. So essentially, my wife took away Layla's fun. She was no longer the boss. The volunteer was.

Your authority is NOT established by your title. It is established using the Trust Equation from Chapter 2 that says trust happens when compassion meets confidence. Trust happens when the trainee feels your compassion for them (you want them to be better) and your confidence in your training,

4. Press and Release

My wife knows that the horse does not respond to her pressure in the round pen. It responds to the *release* of that pressure. She will push the horse to complete the skill by applying pressure from either her presence in its space or a training tool known as a stick until she feels the horse has understood and then will ask her its eyes and "release" the pressure she is applying and allow the horse to rest.

She knows the horse is relaxing when it starts to lick and chew. This is a sign that it has moved to its thinking side of the brain - where learning occurs.

When training people, we apply the same principle. We apply pressure by our placement in the room. For example, if I feel someone is tuning out, I will slowly move to a position right next to them. I never stop talking, so it simply looks like I am moving around the room casually. But the person who is not with me suddenly snaps to it because they know that now that I am standing next to them all eyes are on them.

Another way to apply pressure is through questioning. I love a Socratic approach to training where questions directed to the learner keep their attention and also serve to provide me feedback if they are "getting it" or not. I have a goal for everyone in the room to speak to me at least three times during the session. This may be from me calling on them or from them volunteering an answer. I am conscious of who has participated and who has not. I call on the ones who are not participating and get them engaged. This means that sometimes I ignore a hand raised from someone I have already heard from a couple of times to call on someone I have not.

This technique of questioning or having table discussions or group work are all part of another one of Ron's Principles of Learning - the Principle of Intensity - which says make it an intense learning environment and they will learn more. Nothing is more intense than being put on the spot and having to answer a question in front of the whole room. It keeps you on your toes as a learner.

There is a saying in the horse community - blinking is thinking. Meaning that when the horse is blinking, it is thinking. It's another visual sign of learning the trainer is looking for. You have to do the same as the trainer. Check for comprehension through your questioning. Watch the body language of your trainees. Do you have their eyes?

If you rely on the test at the end of the class to determine learning you are doing it wrong. No offense to teachers in our schools, but the test does not measure learning according to our definition - a change in behavior. Those tests measure memory, not change. You need change to accomplish your goal.

Change doesn't mean your people are bad and need to change. It means they (we) can all get better and advance our skills. Is anyone else frustrated with how fast our world is changing around us? We have to change. We have to learn. We have to be better.

5. Reward their Performance

All of the techniques mentioned above are pressure techniques. I will give you one more in a minute - role play. But in all of these, I am applying pressure to them to get them moving to the thinking side of their brain where the learning occurs. Then, to release pressure, I make sure and reward every performance and every answer.

For example, I might say, good point or right! Very loudly so everyone notices them versus me. I also try to reference answers of students as part of reviewing information using their name as I do. For example, I might say "like Mike said earlier" so Mike gets rewarded (again) for his performance. With each of these techniques, I am rewarding the learner, but I am also releasing the pressure. Just like my wife does with our horse friends. And when you release the pressure, the student responds.

My wife tries to vary the reward each time. She has learned that if they get a treat like an oat snack or peppermint (yes, they like peppermints) that they will only perform when they get that treat. So, she makes sure to vary the reward. Sometimes it is just letting them rest and breathe. Sometimes it is physical touch. In all instances, there is verbal praise for the behavior.

People are no different. They want to be rewarded for their performance. But you need to vary the reward when training. Here is a list of ideas you can use in your training to reward your learners for a job well done.

- Verbal praise: This is as simple as saying, "Hey Catherine, that case study analysis was spot-on. I loved how you connected it to last week's lesson." It's amazing how far a genuine compliment can go.
- Public recognition: Sometimes, sharing someone's success with the group can be really motivating. It could be highlighting great work or mentioning standout contributions during discussions. I often use a person's performance at work as an example of the right way to do it.
- Badges or certificates: People love having something to show for their efforts. Digital badges for online courses or physical certificates for in-person training can be great mementos of achievement. I know it sounds cheesy, but people love badges. Heck, even Jimmy Johns wants to give me a badge for eating the right sandwich.
- Additional responsibilities: For your high performers, consider giving them a chance to lead. Maybe they could run a group project or mentor other learners. Or just have them lead a breakout group when you are doing small group discussion. These are great ways to recognize their skills.
- Small prizes: These don't have to be extravagant. Think along the lines of relevant books, professional development resources, or even some company swag that ties into the training topic. I love the book idea because it is a reward of learning for learning. But honestly, tossing a piece of candy across the room or handing someone a $1 bill has an amazing effect as well.
- Extra breaks or time off: Who doesn't love a bit of bonus free time? An extended lunch break or leaving a bit early can be a great reward for finishing tasks quickly or doing exceptional work.

- Personalized learning paths: For those really excelling, offering chances to explore advanced topics or tackle challenging projects aligned with their interests can be incredibly rewarding.
- Networking opportunities: Giving top performers a chance to connect with industry experts or senior management can be a powerful motivator and learning experience.

6. Repeat

Another principle of learning I got from Ron was the Principle of Exercise. This principle states that people learn best when repetition is used. In other words, a learner needs to hear or do the skill multiple times before they get it.

In my consulting days, I cannot tell you the number of times management was upset at the team for nonperformance or not doing what they were supposed to do. When I asked them about the process of rolling out a new practice or process they would say, "well, I sent an email to everyone and even cc'd the other department heads!"

I love the fact that they add the touch of the cc in their response like that makes all the difference. An email - emphasis on the word *an* as in one. First, how many of us truly read every part of our emails? Second, how many remember every part of our emails? Three, how many remember the last chapter in this book? Get my point?

People need to perform the skill over and over before learning - a change in behavior - occurs. One training session will not suffice. They need to practice. Heads up, another pressure technique coming.

Earlier I said that questioning is a great way to make it an intense learning environment, one of the Principles of Learning. But the best form of Intensity and practice that also has the benefit of checking for comprehension is role play. Wait! Hold up! I don't role play. Did I just read your mind? If not yours, certainly the minds of your trainees (employees.)

<u>Why Role Play is Evil</u>

I like that title because most trainees believe it is evil. They hate it. They make excuses when asked to role play saying, "this is so unnatural. I can do it just fine with a Customer. It's just weird in a class or with you one on one."

Here is the deal. Do you know why your employees say it's sooooo much easier with a Customer versus in front of their peers in a training environment?

Because the Customer does not know that what they just did in the role play sucks!

Your peers know you did bad. They know you do not know what you are doing. There is no way to hide it. So, they make excuses hoping you will buy into their nonsense and cancel the role play. But you are better than that.

Role play is hard. No doubt. Much harder than when you are with a Customer. No doubt. But it is the best way for you to accomplish two very important goals. First, the Repeat step in our process uses role play as a way to live out the Principle of Exercise in learning. Second, you get to check for comprehension. Do they really understand? Typically, a trainer will check for comprehension by asking "any questions?" And, of course, there are none. So obviously they all got it. No worries.

I remember years ago when I was training in the CE industry we were working on Big Screen TVs. Remember those large cabinets that projected the image from beyond onto a 56" screen? If not, they did. Trust me.

One role play, an employee told the "customer" that the big screen had liquid cooling and that meant that a flow of liquid like a waterfall came down the back of the screen while it was on to keep the unit cool and the images bright and sharp. I had to pause for a moment to be sure I heard him right. But yes that is exactly what he said, 'a waterfall of liquid cascading down the back of the screen'.

Here's the thing, he was so believable in his delivery it was scary. And if he had said that to a real Customer (which based on how well tuned this answer was I think he had - many times) the Customer would think that is so cool! I want that in my Big Screen TV. Never mind the fact that water and electricity are not good friends. Could you imagine that Customer explaining to his friends the reason he bought that TV?

Thankfully, we had the roleplay to save us that day. These six important steps in the process are just that - a process. They must ALL be followed for them to work. You must practice them as well. Just like your students need repetition to learn, you do also. It will take you several attempts to get used to these skills. But you can get there. After all, I did!

Here is an axiom for you about role play. The kind you can put on a coffee mug or poster.

Everyone roleplays. They either roleplay with the Customer or they roleplay with you in the class. One version _costs_ you money and the other one _makes_ you money.

So, if you are looking for the reason to roleplay there it is. You can let the student win and not roleplay or let them off the hook with a bad performance, but you are only cheating them and yourself (and your company.) Especially in a sales or Customer experience role within a company, being able to roleplay the techniques is paramount. Like the axion says, they tell you they don't like to roleplay, but they already are.

One tip to help your roleplay sessions work better, after they perform the roleplay, have the class (their peers) provide feedback before you ever say anything. Encourage them to share what they liked about the roleplay and then what the person could do better next time.

First, peers training peers is always the most powerful form of learning. But second, it is not just the person roleplaying who is learning - the class who is asked to provide feedback, is also learning because they are studying what is happening in the roleplay.

Encourage people to "borrow" from roleplays they observe. If they like the way the person phrased it or an example they used, they should add it to their repertoire. You are gaining and learning even while watching if you are doing roleplay correctly.

This training chapter has a lot of ideas for you to improve your people development skills, but the best part is that you can use techniques from this chapter in all parts of your leadership, not just training.

Leading like a Trainer

A good horse trainer, like my wife, understands that her mere presence in the arena communicates volumes to the horse. Every subtle shift in body language, energy, and focus contributes to how the horse perceives and responds to her. This concept of "presence" is equally vital in leadership yet often overlooked in traditional management training.

Here are some ideas to enhance your presence as a trainer or just as a leader.

Cultivate Mindfulness

Before entering important meetings or interactions, take a moment to center yourself. This can help you project calm confidence. Consider implementing a brief meditation or breathing exercise before significant engagements.

Start your day with a 5-minute mindfulness session. Use apps like Headspace or Calm if you need guidance.

Master Body Language

Pay meticulous attention to your posture, gestures, and facial expressions. Aim for open, relaxed body language that conveys confidence and approachability.

- Stand tall with your shoulders back and chin slightly raised to project confidence.
- Use open hand gestures to appear more approachable and honest.
- Make appropriate eye contact to show engagement and build trust.

Energy Management

Be acutely aware of the energy you're bringing into a room. If you're stressed or distracted, take steps to reset before engaging with your team.

- Develop an "energy reset" routine: This could be a quick walk around the office, a moment of deep breathing, or even a power pose in private. (no peacocking)
- Practice emotional intelligence: Learn to recognize and manage your own emotions, and how they affect others.

Present Moment Focus

When interacting with team members, give them your full attention. Put away devices and practice active listening.

- Implement a "devices down" policy during one-on-one meetings and team discussions.
- Practice reflective listening: Paraphrase what you've heard to ensure understanding and show engagement.

Develop Your "Feel

Expert horse trainers often speak of developing a "feel" - an intuitive sense of what the horse needs at any given moment. Leaders can cultivate this by:

- Regularly checking in with team members on both professional and personal levels.
- Paying attention to the overall mood and energy of your team and adjusting your approach accordingly.
- Trusting your instincts about when to push for more and when to ease off.

As you move forward with implementing these strategies, consider the following questions:

1. How can you shift your focus more deliberately from your performance to the learner's needs and potential?
2. In what ways can you better prepare both yourself and your learners for training sessions?
3. How might you incorporate more varied and meaningful rewards into your training approach?
4. What steps can you take to make repetition and roleplay more effective and accepted in your training programs?
5. How can you enhance your presence as a leader and trainer to create a more impactful learning environment?

By addressing these questions and implementing ideas outlined in this chapter, you'll be well on your way to becoming a more effective trainer and leader. Remember, the art of training, whether it's horses or humans, is about building trust, establishing clear communication, and consistently reinforcing desired behaviors. With practice and patience, you can create a learning environment that brings out the best in your team, just like my wife with a rescue horse.

Chapter 6: Shaping the Herd - The Power of Feedback & Rewards

In my study of the complex ecosystem of organizational behavior - corporate culture - one principle reigns supreme: **all behavior is rewarded**. This concept, deceptively simple yet profoundly impactful, forms the bedrock of effective leadership and performance management. What I have learned in my studies of corporate cultures and leadership has been mirrored in watching the horses at our Rescue. All behavior is rewarded there as well.

The truth is that we all have employees that don't do what they are supposed to, and we are left scratching our heads or wringing our hands as we try to get them to change. One of my favorite movie scenes is from <u>A League of Their Own</u>, starring Tom Hanks. In this movie, there is an outfielder who keeps forgetting to throw the ball to the "cut off" man which allows runners to move further around the bases then they should. Hanks, who is struggling with his own "patience" issues calls her over after she messes up yet again, and while he controls his urge to yell and scream at her, you can see the angst throughout his entire body as he says, "you are still not hitting the cutoff man, that is something I would like you to work on." He is shaking so much trying to maintain calm that he must sit down.

I think the reason I like this scene so much is that I can relate. I have felt exactly like that before. So frustrated with an employee who doesn't do what they are supposed to do that I have to sit down. Can you relate?

<u>Coaching versus Leading</u>

In the last chapter, I detailed the difference between teaching and training.

Teaching = passing on knowledge
Training = passing on performance

Each of these is important. Each of these is good. However, to be a trainer means you need to be able to *do* the skill you are training. I can teach you without being able to do it, but I cannot train you.

Think back to our discussion on leader versus manager. Remember the two flipcharts and their definitions? I think we can add a third flipchart and write Coaching on the top of it.

Coaching = motivating performance

Remember our definition of leadership? *Getting others to want to do the things that need to get done.* This doesn't mean that you can do it. Just means you are good at getting others to want to do it. With coaching you are following the same track as Leader, but you are adding two elements for success - motivation and accountability.

I think any good leader would tell you that motivation and accountability are key parts of any leader toolbox, but if you want to see true learning in your team, then you need to focus on coaching.

Learning, by our definition, is a change in behavior. How do we know someone learned? We see a change in their behavior. In school we measure it a bit differently. We use the test grade to determine if you have learned. But in the business world, we are not focused on thought as much as we are on action or behavior.

Consider this, if you are working with an employee, will you consider your work successful if they "tell" you what you want to hear or say the right things? Or will you measure success based on how they behave? Of course, it is the second one.

So, coaching takes on a huge role when we are working with our team and trying to shape their behavior. Now, for clarity, I am not saying you need to be able to be a master at the skill to coach, but you do need to be able to do it yourself.

Horses are funny. They know instantly if the person "training" them has any clue what they are doing. I have watched the horse enter in the round pen for groundwork training and act completely dumb when the trainer gives the command. They are testing the human. Does this human know what they are doing? If not, why am I going to get all sweaty, thinks the horse.

Madison was a yearling that needed groundwork. A volunteer took her into the round pen and tried to get her to move. Madison stared at the volunteer and acted like it had no idea what they were asking. My wife, watching all this take place, steps into the arena and immediately Madison's expression changes. You can see it. She knows the "boss" is here and she means business. With one quick motion, my wife has Madison bounding around the round pen in graceful form.

My wife is a master at groundwork with a horse. She is something to watch. She knows that the definition of learning that applies to people also applies to horses - a change in behavior. But even she gets challenged by some of the rescues that come in. Why? Basically because of the training they have had in the past.

All behavior is rewarded. There I said it again. The horse that is challenging my wife is doing so because this behavior has been rewarded in the past. But who would reward bad behavior, you are asking? We all do.

Ferdinand F. Fournies' work has been a great influence on me and my leadership. In his book, <u>Why Employees Don't Do What They're Supposed to Do and What to Do About It</u>, Fournies delves deep into the root causes of employee nonperformance.

Fournies identified 16 primary reasons why employees don't do what they're supposed to do. And while they are all great, I want to focus on the ones that have had the most impact for me.

They don't know the why
Employees often lack understanding of how their tasks contribute to larger organizational goals. They get that you want it done a certain way, they just do not know why. And horses are the same way.

My wife believes there are two reasons a horse will do what you want them to - one is fear, and the other is respect. You can use either technique to get what you want, but one of them, respect, makes the life of the employee or horse much better.

She chooses respect and this is why her method takes so much longer than other trainers. However, what she knows is that later in that horse's life, it will have many leaders. She wants the horse to approach each one with respect and not with fear. You should have the same mindset. Your job is to grow people for the company. This means they will have multiple leaders as they promote.

The horse also learns from my wife that if they do well, they will be rewarded. Not with treats, but with love and respect in return. And lots of praise. Trets can be used, but honestly, praise and release of pressure is the best reward for a horse.

Clearly communicate the 'why' behind tasks and decisions. Help your team understand the purpose and importance of their work.

They don't know the how
Sometimes, nonperformance is simply due to a lack of knowledge or skills. Just because an employee has been given a job does not mean they know how to do it. Managers are especially bad at relying on titles to determine competency.

If you cannot look yourself in the mirror and guarantee yourself that the employee knows how to do it, then you must give them grace and focus on training. Once you have done this, if the behavior does not change, then you can take a different track.

Invest in comprehensive training programs. Think of how young horses learn from older, more experienced herd members. Create mentorship programs and provide ongoing learning opportunities.

They don't know what
Unclear expectations are a major cause of nonperformance. I have been guilty of this in the past. As a creative personality who likes total ownership of a project, the less direction you give me and the more autonomy you give me, the more I thrive. So, like most leaders, I tend to lead the way I would like to be treated.

I have frustrated many people working for me in my attempt to be "the greatest boss ever." I have learned that most people want direction. They want details and parameters and boundaries. They feel better setup for success if they have that clarity at the beginning. Otherwise, they are not sure what they are doing or truly what you want.

Set clear, specific, and measurable expectations. Just as horses in a herd understand their roles through clear social cues, ensure your team members have a crystal-clear understanding of their responsibilities.

There is no positive consequence to them for doing it

If good performance goes unnoticed, employees may see no reason to put in extra effort. I worked for a manager once that believed your performance review was your paycheck. If you get a paycheck, you are doing a good job. If you do not get a paycheck, then it's because you are fired. No matter how hard I worked my butt (gyat) off, this manager would never tell me "good job". He never showed appreciation for my efforts.

After a while I started noticing that I was working much harder than everyone else and getting the same "reward" - a paycheck. I began to take longer breaks like my colleagues. I began to manage my place in the herd - not trying to lead, just trying to stay in the top 1/3rd where I knew I would not get in trouble, but I also knew I was not giving my best.

Make sure your employees have a positive consequence for performance. The most effective way to reward is through two simple words - thank you! A sincere expression of gratitude - even if the employee is simply doing what they are hired to do - goes a long way in the employee doing what he or she is supposed to do.

Implement a robust recognition system. With the horses, positive behaviors are immediately reinforced through social acceptance and increased status. Similarly, ensure that good performance is promptly and consistently acknowledged. Remember peer recognition is the most powerful.

There is no negative consequence for poor performance

If subpar work is tolerated, it may continue or even increase. I think this is mostly observed on a sales team. Your top sales professional does not get held accountable the way the others do. They have sloppy CRM or lack details for the ops team when the sale is posted for delivery.

In the warehouse, the employee who makes everyone laugh and is the "fun" one shows up late all the time. But he doesn't get in trouble the way the others do.

Address performance issues promptly and consistently. At the rescue, horses will "test" a new volunteer. They want to know if they can boss them around or if they have to do what they say. So, they get into the volunteer's personal space and get pushy. My wife must teach them how to get the horses to back up and obey. If she doesn't catch this early, oftentimes it is too late and no matter what that volunteer does, she has been "marked" by the herd, and they will not listen to her direction. Similarly, don't let poor performance persist without appropriate intervention.

There is a negative consequence to them for doing it

Okay, this one is a blind spot for most managers. We tend to delegate to employees' strengths and not their weaknesses. We want the job done quickly and efficiently and we know which employee can do it, so we ask them each time.

After doing this for a while, the employee starts to think, this sucks! I am the one who always must enter the CRM updates. For me, I saw this when I was a district manager for a retailer back in the day. Visual merchandising was a big thing for our stores. It was one of the things that drove our sales. So obviously, I was very focused on it.

On my team there was a girl named Mackenize who was a visual rockstar. And, naturally, I would put her on this task every time. She would make the coolest displays adding her own touch of flair with extra props that she would bring from home. But I noticed that over time, her displays started looking less amazing and more "check the box done". What I failed to consider was that it was a commission-based sales floor. So, when I had Mackenzie building a display, it actually cost her money. She would make less money that day.

She had a negative consequence for performance. Let that sink in for a minute. Has this ever happened to you? Probably. An employee does exactly what you want, but there is a penalty for doing so. That one is hard. But there is one more that is harder still.

And the number one reason why employees don't do what they are supposed to do is...

They think they are
Sometimes, employees believe they are meeting expectations when they're not. This is the most shocking of them all. An employee genuinely believes he or she is doing a good job. They are not trying to go against you. They honestly have no idea what they are doing is not right.

This happens WAY more than leaders want to admit. Believe me. As a consultant through the years, I would have a front row seat to this. I would get a list of the Right People Right Seats (refer to Jim Collins Good to Great on that one) employees and do my own investigation. The list would be the people that the leader or owner thought needed to go, that they were not the "right" person for the job or company.

I learned early in my career not to trust this - or at least to take it with a grain of salt. More times than I could count, the RPRS list would be very different after my discovery and analysis than what we started with. And this last reason is why. The employee would brag on their efforts, processes or performance. They had no clue their boss thought they were bad. It was sad.

Granted, there were times where the owner was right about the person, but the number of times they were not has always stuck with me. Too many times, a simple alignment conversation between the employee and the leader is all that was needed. Sadly, pride tends to get in the way of this too often.

Provide regular, clear feedback. Like the constant non-verbal communication among rescue horses, maintain ongoing dialogue about performance standards and individual progress. Schedule time to stay aligned. Do your Quarterly Conversations faithfully. This is the way you make this reason - the number one reason why employees don't do what they are supposed to do - is true.

Prescription Without Diagnosis is Malpractice

This is an axiom for physicians and veterinarians alike. There must be a thorough diagnosis or exam before any treatment or prescription can be written. Just as a skilled veterinarian would carefully examine a horse before treatment, leaders must investigate the root causes of employee nonperformance. Remember,

All Behavior is Rewarded!

Your non-action can say as much as your reaction.

Let that one sink in. (Lots of sinking in this chapter.)

Why do I mention this? We just covered some of the top reasons why, but, if we are honest, much of what you read happens inadvertently. Meaning that you did not intend to reward the behavior, but you did. For example, here are some ways you might be inadvertently rewarding behavior without realizing it.

Attention as a Reward

Leaders and managers often give more attention to underperformers, trying to help them improve. However, this attention can be perceived as a reward, reinforcing the undesired behavior. I know that may sound crazy, but any parent reading this right now just resonated with that thought.

In the book, Teamwork, by Pat Riley, he discusses his Teamwork acronym. Pat Riley, a highly successful basketball coach at all levels, said that one of his secrets to success was that he treated all players equally. This was the "e" in Teamwork.

He explained that treating them equally did not mean treating them the same. In other words, he wasn't treating all his players identically, but he was treating them equally. He related a story about a team he had that had a rookie player and a veteran (future hall of fame) player as part of the starting lineup. He would spend 30 minutes with the rookie covering basic fundamentals of the game. This Is what that player needed. But to be "equal" he would spend 30 minutes with the veteran player. Only with the veteran he would not focus on fundamentals, he focused on praise. That is what this player needed - to be reinforced verbally that he was one of the greatest players of all time.

My wife often comes home frustrated by this principle. She wholeheartedly agrees with it, but some days she just cannot provide equal time with horses. She always prioritizes the rescues working toward a forever home than the permanent residents, like Cletus, her heart horse, who live on the ranch as well. She often feels like she has cheated her heart horse with all the attention the rescues get. She must be deliberate in making time for him to protect against this principle affecting the herd.

Consider how you treat your team equally. And don't let this behavior reward impact the success of your team. Balance your attention. Ensure high performers receive equal or greater attention for their positive contributions.

Lowering Standards

Over time, managers might lower their expectations for underperforming employees, which is a form of reward for poor performance. I know I have done this in my career. I just get tired of fighting it, so I lower what I expect.

I was leading a retail division of store managers who had not had any KPIs assigned to them before. As I started rolling out this principle, I got a ton of pushback. I heard things like "my metrics were not fair." or "they were too hard." At least that is what they all cried out.

And they did have a vested interest, I tied their "up until that point free bonus" to the new KPIs. Meaning that if they did not achieve the KPI, they did not get a bonus. Whereas before they simply got the bonus for showing up after the quarter was over. Well, I guess they also didn't steal anything, but other than that it was really just salary.

The KPIs were tough. One metric I started tracking had been tracked before, just not with any intention. When I arrived, the metric was at 8%. I set the company standard to 30%. So, you can understand why I had a revolt.

I cannot tell you how many conversations I had with leaders, HR, anyone who would listen to the managers to change or lower my standards - especially this one. But after two years, we were at that 30%. Where would we have been if I had lowered it? Better than 8%? Sure. But is better what you want? Or is best what you desire?

Maintain consistent standards. Like the unchanging laws of nature that govern a horse herd, your performance standards should remain constant and apply equally to all team members.

Failure to Provide Feedback

When managers avoid giving negative feedback, employees may assume their performance is acceptable. This is a big one. People hate confrontation. I know I don't relish it. And I am not sure I trust someone who does either.

This will play itself out within your team. Everyone's watching to see what you do. If someone comes in late and you do nothing, then they all assume it's okay to come in late. Sometimes when my wife goes to feed, the horses are in the wrong stalls. The easiest thing to do is simply let them stay and eat. But if she does, then the horse learns that it does not matter anymore, and they stop caring. They have assigned stalls for a reason. Different stalls have different setups and accommodations. We do not have a "one stall that fits all" barn. So, it does matter which stall the horse goes in.

Provide timely, specific feedback. In a horse herd, feedback is immediate and clear. Strive to emulate this in your leadership style.

Remote Shaping

The shift towards remote work has presented new challenges in shaping organizational behavior. Without the immediate feedback and social cues present in an office environment, intentional effort is required to reinforce desired behaviors.

Consider these strategies:

1. Virtual recognition platforms: Implement digital tools that allow for public recognition of good work. This can help replicate the social reinforcement that occurs naturally in an office setting.
2. Regular video check-ins: Use video calls not just for task-related communication, but also for providing feedback and recognition. The visual element can make the reinforcement more impactful.
3. Clear performance metrics: With less direct oversight, it's crucial to have clear, measurable indicators of good performance. This allows for more objective and consistent reinforcement.
4. Virtual team-building activities: Create opportunities for social learning and peer recognition in a remote setting through virtual team events.
5. Asynchronous feedback tools: Implement systems that allow for immediate feedback even when team members are working at different times.

Timing is Everything

In both horse training and organizational leadership, the timing of reinforcement is crucial. The closer the reinforcement is to the desired behavior, the stronger the association between the two.

With horses, if the feedback is not immediate, they will disconnect from it. Especially if you are trying to correct. You cannot go into a stall that has been trashed by a horse and then go yell at it in the pasture. It thinks you're crazy.

After a session of groundwork training. My wife will often tether the horse to a patience pole This is simply a pole we installed in the shade that she ties them to. It allows movement around the pole without restriction, but they cannot leave that immediate area. The horse is left to think and consider the training (behaviors) it just worked on. As it thinks about it, it helps solidify the behavior she is looking for from the horse. It is immediate and timely.

In an organizational context, immediate reinforcement isn't always possible, but leaders should strive to provide feedback and recognition as close to the desired behavior as possible. This might mean:

1. Providing real-time feedback during or immediately after presentations or client interactions.
2. Implementing systems for peer recognition that allow for immediate acknowledgment of good work.
3. Having daily or weekly check-ins to discuss recent performance rather than waiting for monthly or quarterly reviews.
4. Using digital tools that allow for quick, public recognition of achievements.

Remember, delayed reinforcement is better than no reinforcement, but immediate reinforcement is the most powerful in shaping behavior.

One rule to follow here, criticize in private and praise in public. I wish I could remember who said that first and give them their proper credit. I wish I was the one who said it first. But I have always tried to follow this advice because it is so spot on.

Don't Be an Over Rewarder

While consistent positive reinforcement is crucial, it's equally important to avoid the pitfall of over rewarding. With horses, my wife varies the reward. Sometimes there are treats involved, but the majority of the time it is simply praise and touch. She doesn't give a treat for a big behavior and a "good job" for a little one. The horse will never know what "reward" is coming, but it knows one is if it behaves properly. Horses are prey animals and when they are under stress from training, they are not thinking about food like a dog might.

When every action is met with lavish praise or rewards, several negative consequences can occur:

1. Diminished impact: The power of rewards can diminish when they're given too frequently or for minimal effort. This is like how a horse might become "treat-wise" and start performing behaviors only when they know a treat is available.
2. Entitlement mentality: Employees may begin to expect rewards for simply doing their job, rather than for going above and beyond.
3. Decreased intrinsic motivation: Over reliance on external rewards can actually decrease internal motivation to perform well.
4. Reduced quality: If employees are rewarded regardless of the quality of their work, there's little incentive to strive for excellence.

To avoid these pitfalls, try these ideas.

- Vary your rewards and recognition: Sometimes a simple "thank you" is sufficient, while other times a more substantial acknowledgment might be appropriate. Try a handwritten note for impact for example.
- Be specific in your praise: Instead of general compliments, tie your recognition to specific behaviors or outcomes.
- Set clear standards: Ensure your team understands what level of performance is expected as part of their regular duties, and what constitutes going above and beyond.
- Focus on progress and effort: Recognize improvement and hard work, not just outcomes.
- Use a mix of individual and team-based rewards: This can help foster both personal accountability and teamwork.

I have seen leaders get in trouble being an "over rewarder" or "over praiser." Everyone wants to work for a positive leader. We love to get praise for a job well done. But I have seen leaders who focus so much on praise and celebration in public that the effect starts to wear off. And worse, the impact is like the old adage that if everything is important then nothing is important.

Here we are saying if all we do is share positively - even in a down sales month - then our employees become de-synthesized and a little disconnected. I remember a leader giving an award to an employee for their rock star performance and many people in the room thinking, why this guy? The CEO is praising them, and the other employees are thinking "this guy is the worst person on the team. They make my job difficult, and they make my job harder."
The CEO's heart was in the right place, but in over rewarding, it had a negative impact on the team.

The principle that all behavior is rewarded is not just a theoretical concept—it's a powerful tool for leadership and organizational transformation. By understanding the nuances of how rewards shape behavior, both in horse herds and human organizations, leaders can create environments that naturally cultivate high performance and engagement.

As you consider the ideas in this chapter, use these questions to craft your strategy:

1. How can you implement a more effective reward system that reinforces desired behaviors and performance in your organization?
2. In what ways can you improve your feedback mechanisms to ensure timely and specific recognition of both positive and negative behaviors?
3. How might you adjust your leadership approach to avoid inadvertently rewarding undesired behaviors or creating negative consequences for good performance?

4. What steps can you take to better align your team's understanding of expectations with your actual performance standards?
5. How can you create a culture where coaching and motivation are integrated into daily operations, rather than being seen as separate activities?

As you move forward in your leadership journey, challenge yourself to become a master observer and shaper of behavior. Like a skilled horse trainer or a wise boss mare, your ability to consistently reinforce desired behaviors while redirecting unproductive ones will determine the success and harmony of your organizational "herd."

Remember, every interaction, every decision, and every moment of attention is a form of reward. Use these moments wisely, and you'll create a thriving, high-performing team that moves together with the grace and power of a well-coordinated horse herd.

Chapter 7: Unleashing Innovation: Lessons from Free-Spirited Horses

So, Layla Rose Ranch is a horse rescue. Hopefully by now you know that. 90% of the horses we take in are not wild. But every now and then, we do get an unhandled mustang off the plains. And you can see a big difference in these horses for sure. These horses have a unique spirit that makes you think of the Wild West for sure.

In the untamed wildernesses of America, wild horses roam freely, embodying a spirit of freedom, adaptability, and innovation that has allowed them to thrive for centuries. These horses, unfettered by human constraints, can also teach us some lessons - especially when it comes to innovation.

So, let's leave our ranch for this chapter and head West to the world of wild horses roaming free in herds on the plains of Idaho. And I know as you read some of these ideas, you will roll your eyes and think "I wish we could do that!" And that is okay. I get that not all companies are based in the Silicon Valley or in the tech world with incredible margins. Try to keep an open mind, though, and look for the ideas that do fit.

The Power of Unfettered Thinking

Wild horses, free from the confines of stables and human-imposed routines, exhibit remarkable adaptability. They navigate diverse terrains, from arid deserts to lush mountain meadows, constantly adjusting their behavior to survive and thrive. This adaptability is the cornerstone of their success and offers a powerful metaphor for innovation in the business world.

Here are some ideas to help you start building innovation into your company DNA. Not all will work for your company, after all, margins are very different between businesses. But hopefully, you can pick up a couple of ideas as you read through.

Encourage Exploration
- Implement "innovation time" where employees can work on projects of their choosing, like Google's famous 20%-time policy.
- Create an "idea sandbox" where team members can experiment with new concepts without the pressure of immediate results.
- Establish an "innovation grant" program where employees can pitch ideas and receive resources to explore them.

Adapt to Change
- Conduct regular "environmental scans" to identify industry shifts and emerging trends.
- Implement agile methodologies across departments, not just in IT, to increase organizational flexibility.
- Develop scenario planning exercises to prepare for various future possibilities.

I honestly thought that after COVID, our lives would go back to "normal." But we have a new normal don't we? And the change is still happening. So, making your company okay with adaptability is a good thing.

Now keep in mind we are not say change to change. I am not talking about internal changes as much as being able to adapt to external changes or pressures pushing in on your business.

Even with our horse rescue, a 5019(c)3 charity, we have had to adapt our fundraising. Some bad actors came into the space that were raising tons of money to rescue horses - except that they weren't. they were buying trucks and paying themselves big salaries. It has made people cautious about supporting horse rescues. And we understand and actually respect that. But the rescue survives on donations. So, we have had to adapt and innovate. I would like to think this book is such an innovation.

Leverage Natural Instincts

- Use personality assessments like Lenconi's Work Geniuses or StrengthsFinder to identify team members' innate strengths and align them with innovation initiatives.
- Create cross-functional "innovation swat teams" that bring together diverse natural talents to tackle complex problems.
- Implement a "strength-based" approach to project assignments, allowing team members to gravitate towards roles that align with their instincts.

Consider how Netflix has embodied the wild horse mindset in its business evolution. Starting as a DVD-by-mail service, the company has repeatedly adapted to changing market conditions. When streaming technology emerged, Netflix didn't cling to its existing model but boldly pivoted, eventually becoming the world's leading streaming platform. More recently, they've adapted again by creating original content, competing directly with traditional studios and networks.

This willingness to explore new territories, adapt to technological changes, and leverage their strengths in content delivery showcases the power of the wild horse mindset in action.

Conversely, consider Blockbuster's lack of innovation. Did you know that Marc Randolph, the co-founder of Netflix and its first CEO, tried to sell Netflix to Blockbuster? They turned him down flat, preferring to focus on brick-and-mortar rentals. Today, there is only one Blockbuster store left in the US, and it is an Airbnb.

Harnessing the Power of the Collective

While we often think of wild horses as free-spirited individuals, mostly because they are, they do function as a cohesive herd, leveraging collective intelligence for survival and success. This balance between individuality and collective action provides a powerful model for innovative teams in the business world.

Here are some strategies for implementing innovation:

Create Innovation Tiger Teams

- Establish cross-functional innovation teams that meet regularly to brainstorm and develop new ideas.
- Implement a rotating leadership model within these teams to ensure diverse perspectives guide the process.
- Use collaborative tools like Miro or Mural to facilitate virtual ideation sessions.

Implement Cross-Functional Projects

- Launch "innovation challenges" that require collaboration between different departments.
- Create a "department swap" program where employees work in different areas of the business for short periods. (Similar to the "experience day" idea from Chapter 1.)
- Establish an "innovation mentor" system pairing employees from different functions.

Celebrate Collective Achievements

- Implement a points-based reward system for collaborative innovations.
- Host quarterly "innovation showcases" where teams present their collaborative projects.
- Create an "innovation wall of fame" in your office or virtual workspace highlighting successful team efforts.
- People love money, so make sure they can get some money or something desirable for their points.

I first learned about W.L. Gore & Associates, the company behind Gore-Tex, when I was working in the footwear industry. This company has long been recognized for its innovative, lattice-like organizational structure that mimics the collective intelligence of a herd. The company operates without traditional hierarchies, job titles, or chains of command. Instead, employees (called "associates") self-organize into teams based on projects and interests.

This structure allows for rapid formation of cross-functional teams to address new challenges or opportunities, much like how a herd of wild horses might quickly reorganize to face a threat or exploit a new food source. The result is a company culture that has consistently landed Gore on lists of the most innovative companies in the world.

The Power of Play in Innovation

Young horses in the wild exhibit boundless curiosity and playfulness. This natural inclination to explore, experiment, and learn through play is at the heart of innovation. By fostering a similar spirit of playful curiosity in your organization, you can unlock new realms of creativity and innovation.

Here are some ideas to help you foster a culture of curiosity.

Allocate Time for Play

- Implement "Creative Fridays" where team members can work on passion projects or learn new skills.
- Create a "play budget" for each department to use on team-building and creative activities.
- Design office spaces with game rooms or creativity zones to encourage playful thinking.

Encourage Question-Asking

- Start meetings with a "question of the day" to spark curiosity and discussion.
- Implement a "no-stupid-questions" policy to create a safe space for inquiry.
- Create a company-wide "question board" where employees can post and answer each other's queries. No better resource than your peers.

Provide Resources for Learning

- Offer a learning stipend for employees to take courses or attend conferences of their choice.
- Create a company library (physical or digital) filled with diverse resources. We did this at my last company, and it was amazing to see the faces of recruits when we were giving them a tour of our offices and told them about the library. We had two bookcases. One said To Keep and one said To Borrow.
- Host regular "lunch and learn" sessions where employees can share knowledge on various topics.

IDEO, the global design company, is renowned for its playful approach to innovation. The company's offices are filled with toys, prototyping materials, and spaces designed to inspire creativity. IDEO encourages its employees to engage in playful exploration as part of the design process.

For instance, when tasked with redesigning the shopping cart, IDEO's team began by playing with existing carts in the parking lot, observing how children interacted with them, and rapidly prototyping wild ideas. This playful approach led to a revolutionary design that addressed pain points no one had previously considered.

Finding the Innovation Sweet Spot

In a wild horse herd, the lead stallion provides necessary structure and protection while allowing for individual freedom. This delicate balance is crucial for innovation in business as well. Leaders must create an environment that offers enough structure to guide efforts effectively, but enough freedom to allow for creative thinking and risk-taking.

This part of innovation is truly more of a balancing act. It is possible to go too far with innovation and lose the important day to day function focus of your company. So here are some ideas for your "balancing act."

Set Clear Objectives
- Use the OKR (Objectives and Key Results) framework to set clear goals while allowing flexibility in execution. These are not Goals. Goals are different. These are objectives which are more focused on purpose.
- Implement a "purpose alignment model" to ensure innovation efforts are tied to company objectives.
- Conduct regular "innovation alignment" sessions to keep creative efforts on track with business goals. Remember, innovation is fun. So, employees will tend to want to spend as much time on that as they

can. But you also have a business to run. So, this last idea helps control that.

This first idea is important because I often see misalignment with employees and leadership when it comes to the topic of innovation. An employee might think that innovation is "fun" time with no real purpose other than being a cool place to work and a way to release the pressures of day-to-day operations and activities.
Whereas leadership sees it as an investment in the future growth of the company. These next ideas will help with that alignment but still need close attention to be done effectively.

Establish Innovation Parameters

- Create an "innovation SOW" that outlines the scope, resources, and constraints for projects.
- Implement a stage/gate process for innovation projects with clear criteria for moving forward.
- Develop an "innovation playbook" that outlines best practices and methodologies while encouraging creative approaches.

Implement Flexible Work Structures

- Adopt a results-only work environment (ROWE) where employees are evaluated on output, not hours worked. This helps keep the time in check.
- Implement a "flextime" policy allowing employees to work when they feel most creative. For example, I am not a morning person at all. So don't ask me to be innovative or creative at 8:00am - won't happen.
- Create "focus zones" and "collaboration zones" in the office to accommodate different work styles and needs.

3M, a company known for innovations like Post-it Notes and Scotch Tape, has long had a policy allowing employees to spend 15% of their time on projects of their own choosing. This policy provides a structure for innovation (a set amount of time) while offering freedom in how that time is used.

The result has been a continuous stream of innovations, with products developed during this 15%-time accounting for a significant portion of 3M's revenue. This approach demonstrates how providing structure (dedicated time) and freedom (choice of project) can lead to significant innovations.

Designing Environments that Inspire

Wild horses thrive in open spaces where they can roam freely. Similarly, innovation flourishes in environments that provide both physical and mental space for creativity. The design of your workspace and the creation of mental space for your team can significantly impact their innovative output.

Here are some ideas to consider to help you design for innovation.

Create Collaborative Spaces
- Design office layouts with flexible, modular furniture that can be easily rearranged for different types of collaboration. My daughters' middle school changes the classroom layout each 9-week grading period. It stimulates the mind by moving the child and the room around.
- Implement "collision zones" - areas designed to increase chance encounters between employees from different departments.
- Create themed ideation rooms (e.g., a "forest room" or "space room") to inspire different thinking patterns. This one is a bit out there, I know. But we all know that being immersed in a space is the best way to get the creative juices flowing.

Provide Quiet Zones

- Designate "silent areas" for deep, focused work. And this doesn't mean a repurposed closet.
- Offer bookable "creativity pods" for individual ideation sessions.
- Implement a "library hour" policy where the entire office maintains quiet for focused work. This is great if there is no extra space available to separate for quiet. No music. No phones.

The quiet idea is important. Some people on your team just don't have the innovation bug. They don't connect with it and don't want any part of it. So, a bunch of employees yapping excitedly about new ideas can be chaos for them in the work environment. Protect your non-innovators as well.

Embrace Virtual Spaces

- Utilize virtual reality platforms for immersive brainstorming sessions, especially for remote teams.
- Create a digital "innovation hub" where employees can share ideas, collaborate on projects, and access resources. This can be a simple intranet site. Microsoft and Google both have these as part of their offerings.
- Implement AI-powered ideation tools to help spark new ideas and connections.

You cannot have younger daughters and not know about Pixar. Pixar's studio in Emeryville, California, is a testament to the power of thoughtful space design in fostering innovation. The central atrium, known as The Steve Jobs Building, was specifically designed to encourage chance encounters between employees from different departments.

The building includes numerous collaborative spaces, from cafes to screening rooms, alongside quiet areas for focused work. This balance of open, collaborative spaces and areas for individual focus has been credited with fostering the creativity that has made Pixar a leader in animated storytelling.

<u>Embracing the Iterative Nature of Innovation</u>

Wild horses are constantly on the move, adapting their journey based on the resources and challenges they encounter. This iterative process is crucial in innovation, where the path from idea to successful implementation is rarely straight.

I know iterative is a big word. And not trying to be trendy. At least it's not Gen A slang. (You Sigma parents know what I mean.) Here are some ideas for implementing an iterative approach at your workspace.

Encourage Rapid Prototyping
- Adopt a "fail fast, learn fast" mentality by creating low-fidelity prototypes early in the process.
- Implement "innovation sprints" - short, focused periods of intense work on a specific problem or idea.
- Use 3D printing and other rapid prototyping technologies to quickly bring ideas into physical form. These devices are surprisingly cheap and available at a local woodworking store.

Embrace Failure as Learning
- Create a "Didn't Work Wall" where teams can share lessons from unsuccessful projects. You might like
- Host an "Oops Nights" where team members share stories of failures and what they learned.
- Implement a "no-blame" policy for innovative projects that don't succeed. (We will discuss the blameless problem-solving idea in the

next chapter.) Innovation does not yield to success quite often and that's okay.

Implement Feedback Loops
- Use techniques like "innovation poker" where team members can bet on or against ideas to gather honest feedback.
- Implement regular "pivot or persevere" meetings to assess the progress of innovation projects.
- Create an "innovation board" of diverse stakeholders to provide ongoing feedback on projects.

Amazon's approach to innovation, encapsulated in Jeff Bezos's "Day 1" philosophy, emphasizes the importance of maintaining a start-up mentality even as a large corporation. This approach involves rapid prototyping, embracing failure, and constant iteration.

For instance, Amazon's development of the Kindle involved numerous iterations and failures before arriving at a successful product. The company's willingness to experiment, fail, and learn quickly has been a key factor in its ability to innovate across diverse sectors, from e-commerce to cloud computing.

What Would Steve Jobs Do?

Whenever I take on a new role at a company, I always try to embody Steve Jobs' approach to innovation. In the book Chasing Cool, by Noah Kerner and Gene Pressman, they set out to help you answer the question "how do you become the iPod of your industry?" The authors note that Steve Jobs took a different approach when creating the iPod.

At the time, the Sony Walkman (I had one of course as did about 80% of the world) dominated the marketplace. For those younger leaders reading, the Sony Walkman was the premier way you listened to music portably - meaning you attached the Walkman to your belt and put on your headphones and this battery-operated miracle would play your favorite FM station or your favorite cassette tape. Some of them even played BOTH sides of the cassette tape without having to remove it and turn it over! I know that is exciting isn't it.

When Steve Jobs wanted to take Apple into this portable music space, he didn't take the traditional approach. Most companies would buy a Walkman and disassemble it to see what made it so great. They would try to innovate the device into something better or "cooler" as the authors term it.

But that's not what Steve Jobs did. Instead, he asked the question, "how can we change the way people experience music?" And from this approach, the iPod was born. And truthfully, it launched a whole new world of technology that changed all our lives forever.

As you are preparing your company and culture for innovation, think like Steve Jobs. Yes, he was not a pleasant man to work with. But his approach of focusing on the experience versus the device is what set Apple apart from everyone else. And you can do that too. Be the disruptor in your industry. Video killed the radio star.

By embracing the free-spirited nature of wild horses (and Steve Jobs), you can create an environment where innovation thrives. Remember, like a herd of wild horses, your organization has the potential to adapt, create, and excel in even the most challenging business landscapes.

As you move forward, consider how you can incorporate these wild horse-inspired strategies into your leadership approach:

1. How can you create more space - both physical and mental - for creativity in your organization?
2. In what ways can you better balance structure and freedom to foster innovation?
3. How might you encourage more playfulness and curiosity among your team members?
4. What steps can you take to improve collaborative innovation across different departments?
5. How can you make your innovation process more iterative and responsive to feedback?

And last, and most importantly,

0. How can we build or be the iPod of our industry?

By answering these questions and implementing some of the ideas from this chapter, you'll be well on your way to leading a more innovative, adaptable, and successful organization. Like a herd of wild horses roaming the open plains, your team will be equipped to navigate the ever-changing business landscape with agility, creativity, and collective intelligence.

Remember, innovation is not just about generating new ideas - it's about creating an environment where those ideas can flourish and be transformed into reality. By fostering a wild horse mentality in your leadership approach, you can unleash the full innovative potential of your organization and lead it to new heights of success.

Chapter 8: Ethical Leadership in a Global Paddock

If you work with horses much at all, you will notice that each herd - no matter how big or small - has its own dynamics, but the most successful ones always have one thing in common: strong, ethical leadership. The boss mare (or stallion), often not the youngest or strongest, guides the herd with wisdom, integrity, and a keen sense of what's best for the group. As we navigate the complex world of global business, there's a lot we can learn from these noble steeds.

In today's interconnected - meaning everyone knows everyone's business thanks to the internet and social media - business landscape, ethical leadership is more crucial than ever. We're no longer just dealing with the local paddock; we're navigating a vast, global field where our actions can have far-reaching consequences.

I know some of you might be thinking, "Ethical leadership sounds great, but in the real world, it's not always that simple." And you're right. It's not simple. But neither is leading a herd through challenging terrains and unpredictable weather. Yet, lead mares do it every day. The key is commitment, consistency, and a clear vision of what's best for the entire herd.

Before we dive into practical strategies, let's take a moment to understand what ethical leadership really means, through the lens of our rescue horse friends.

In a herd, the boss mare isn't chosen for her strength or speed, but for her wisdom and ability to make decisions that benefit the entire group. She doesn't rule through force or domination (although she does get aggressive at times), but through trust and respect earned over time. Her actions consistently demonstrate care for the herd's wellbeing, even at personal cost.

Similarly, in the business world, ethical leaders are those who consistently make decisions based on what's right, not just what's profitable or expedient. They consider the impact of their choices on all stakeholders - employees, customers, shareholders, the community, and the environment.

Key traits of ethical leaders, inspired by boss mares:

- Integrity: Always acting in alignment with their values, even when no one is watching.
- Fairness: Treating all members of the herd equally and making decisions without favoritism.
- Responsibility: Taking ownership of decisions and their consequences.
- Transparency: Being open about decision-making processes and rationales.
- Long-term perspective: Considering the future impact of current decisions.

Navigating Ethical Dilemmas with the integrity of Shelby

When faced with a challenging situation, Shelby, the boss mare at Layla Rose Ranch doesn't panic or shy away. Instead, she approaches each hurdle with steady determination, guided by her instincts and experience. As leaders, we need to approach ethical dilemmas with the same resolve.

With so many horses coming and going from all different breeds, shapes and sizes, the rescue can be a chaotic place for a horse herd. We have rescued off-the-track thoroughbreds in the Secretariat line, wild mustangs from the Navajo reservation, a giant draft horse and a 100lb miniature horse named Magic just to name a few.

This constant state of change can be rough on anyone or any horse, but Shelby handles it with grace. (Most days that is) She is always cautious and tests the new arrivals. She wants to know if they present a threat or benefit to her herd. Cletus joins in as well. As the lead male, he is more concerned with the protection of the herd than the harmony like Shelby.

Here are some ideas to help you navigate ethical challenges at your company.

Develop Your Moral Compass
- Create a personal ethical code that aligns with your values and your organization's mission. Revisit and refine this code regularly.
- Regularly reflect on your decisions and their ethical implications. Consider keeping an "ethics journal" to track your thoughts and growth over time. Remember, every decision you make is precedent that can be cited later.
- Seek out mentors known for their integrity and learn from their experiences. Just as young horses learn from older ones, we can learn from those who've successfully navigated ethical challenges before.
- Study ethical frameworks and philosophies to broaden your understanding of ethical reasoning.

Practice Ethical Decision-Making
- Implement an ethical decision-making framework in your organization. For example, Is it legal? Is it fair? How would I feel if this decision was made public? How would it impact the most vulnerable members of our "herd"?
- Role-play ethical dilemmas in team meetings to build "ethical muscle memory." Use real-world scenarios relevant to your industry.
- Establish an ethics committee or advisory board to provide guidance on complex ethical issues.
- Create an ethics hotline or anonymous reporting system for employees to raise concerns without fear of retaliation. Make sure

anyone using it knows the safeguards put into place to suppress retaliation against them.

Lead with Transparency

- Communicate the reasoning behind difficult decisions, especially when they involve ethical considerations. Be as open as a boss mare is with her herd.
- Be open about mistakes and how you're addressing them. Remember, even the wisest boss mares sometimes make errors in judgment.
- Share ethical success stories to reinforce positive behaviors and show that ethical decisions can lead to positive outcomes.
- Hold regular "ethical town halls" where employees can ask questions and discuss ethical concerns openly. On this one, I would not recommend adding another meeting per se but rather add a section to your monthly all-hands meetings. Consistently talking about ethics and integrity is how to weave it into your company culture.

Consider how Patagonia, the outdoor clothing company, has embodied this approach. When they discovered their supply chain included farms that were practicing "mulesing" (a cruel practice in wool production), they didn't try to hide it. Instead, they openly acknowledged the issue, severed ties with those suppliers, and worked to develop more ethical alternatives. This transparency and commitment to their values has strengthened their brand and customer loyalty.

Conversely, think about the numerous companies that have tried to cover up ethical breaches, only to face much bigger scandals when the truth came out. It's like a herd following a leader who's lost their way - sooner or later, the entire group will find themselves in danger.

Building a Culture of Trust and Reliability

With horses, trust is everything. Herd members rely on each other for safety, companionship, and guidance. A reliable leader keeps the herd safe and united. In the same way, ethical leaders build organizations where trust and reliability are the foundation of every interaction.

With each rescue horse we bring in, the most difficult part can be the rebuilding of trust - even more so than its medical care. As I have shared, a horse we are dealing with at the Rescue comes with a past full of abuse or neglect. These animals have been discarded by their owners and given up for slaughter.

Because of its past, the horse has a hard time with trust, not only with humans, but also with the other horses at the Rescue. And, sadly even with themselves. After all, they have no idea how they ended up with a tag on their hide scheduled for auction. It can take a month to gain their trust again. Sure, you can get a horse to do what you want through force, but that doesn't build trust does it?

A friend of my wife who runs an animal sanctuary told us a story about her grandfather and his horse. There was a wildfire sweeping through their land and her grandfather was stuck on one side of the line of the fire. The only way to survive was to go through the flames to the other side where it was safe. As the flames were closing in, he mounted his trusted horse and because of the adrenaline of the situation, he spurred the horse much harder than normal. This made the horse rear, and her grandfather fell off.

The horse plunged into and through the flames to the other side. When it got to safety, it realized its rider was not on its back. So, what did that horse do? It went back through the flames and got him. And then brought him through the flames yet again to safety.

Her grandfather survived that day because of the bond of trust between horse and rider. Between leader and follower.

Here are some ideas for building this culture of trust in your company. While the idea alone is not enough to change a culture, consistent use of the idea over time will begin to program change into it.

Lead by Example
- Consistently demonstrate ethical behavior, especially when it's difficult. Like a boss mare who chooses a safer but longer route, show that you're willing to make tough choices for the greater good.

I had a boss that exemplified this. Coleman was the CEO at my last company where I served as his right hand as the CXO. Although younger than me, his ethical compass was an example for me and even motivated me to be more like him. Which was a very good thing. I remember the first time I saw it demonstrated. He found an error in the calculation a vendor had made on *their* invoice to us.

Now the truth is, the vendor who sent it didn't know, and, in fact, no one would have ever noticed or cared. It was a $5,000 error from months ago. The vendor had already closed its books. Which is how we knew they didn't even know it. He contacted the vendor, told them of their mistake and sent a check for the difference that very day.

- Own up to your mistakes quickly and publicly. This vulnerability builds trust and encourages others to be honest as well.

This one is hard to do for us prideful leaders. Maybe it's just a male thing, but I know for me this is very hard. I want people to think I am great so they will follow my lead. I worry that if I make a mistake they will lose faith and trust in me. And therefore, not want to follow me. Sound familiar?

I make a practice to openly share my errors or mistakes with my team. I even practice the same with my girls at home. I have three middle school daughters. And more than one time, I have had to sit down and apologize to them for my behavior. As a dad, I can overreact sometimes. I know dads are reading this and thinking "what?" And moms are reading this thinking "preach!" But if my job is to disciple my girls well, then admitting my mistakes openly with them is important. Unfortunately, they tend to like to hear my "mistake" stories from my growing up way too much!

- Celebrate ethical decisions made by team members, even if they resulted in short-term losses. This reinforces the importance of ethical behavior throughout the organization.

Yes, I did share with the entire company what their CEO did in contacting that vendor and sending them a check. I wanted them to know what ethics looked like in our company, but also for them to see ethics being lived out by their leaders. (Remember, lead by example).

- Be visible and accessible. Just as the boss mare is always present and aware of her herd's needs, make sure you're not an absent or distant leader.

Foster Open Communication

- Implement a "no retaliation" policy for those who raise ethical concerns. This creates a safe environment for honest dialogue.
- Hold regular "ethics roundtables" where employees can discuss ethical challenges they're facing. This collective problem-solving mimic how herds work together to overcome obstacles.
- Create an "ethical dilemma of the month" newsletter to keep ethics top-of-mind and encourage ongoing discussions.
- Encourage cross-departmental communication to ensure ethical considerations are shared across the organization.

Build Ethics into Your Processes

- Include ethical conduct in performance reviews and promotion criteria. Make it clear that success in your organization means more than just hitting financial targets.
- Develop a comprehensive ethics training program that goes beyond compliance. Include scenario-based learning and discussions of real-world ethical dilemmas.
- Create an ethics committee to oversee and guide the organization's ethical practices. Ensure this committee has real power to influence decisions.
- Implement ethical audits alongside financial audits to regularly assess your organization's ethical health.

I first met Tony Hsieh at the end of 1999. His incubator had just launched Zappos.com and was struggling to make it work. They were having a hard time getting people to want to buy shoes online versus in brick-and-mortar stores as they had done their entire lives.

During my time consulting with Tony and Zappos, I came to know a person who was as "outside the box" as you could get. (In this case a shoebox.) He took that small startup and sold it to Amazon for $1 Billion. So, I would say that that was some proof that he knew what he was doing.

Today, everyone knows the Zappos brand. And thanks to the leadership and culture, they sell lots more than shoes. Zappos is renowned for its strong culture of trust and reliability. Their core values, which include "Deliver WOW Through Service" and "Build Open and Honest Relationships With Communication," aren't just words on a wall. They live every day through their policies and practices. For instance, their Customer service reps are empowered to make decisions that benefit the customer, even if it might cost the company in the short term. This trust in their employees builds a culture of reliability that extends to their Customers.

The Global Paddock: Ethical Leadership Across Cultures

Just as different herds might have slightly different social norms, different cultures have varying perspectives on ethics and leadership. Navigating this global paddock requires sensitivity, adaptability, and a strong ethical core.

Disclaimer here, I have not personally been part of leading the merger of two foreign companies but have with two domestic companies. I have a friend who handles the monumental task of bringing a US company together with a foreign company in mergers and acquisitions. His insight and counsel sparked the ideas in this next section.

Here are some ideas for ethical leadership in a global context:

Develop Cultural Intelligence
- Provide comprehensive cross-cultural training for all employees, especially those in leadership positions. This should go beyond

surface-level cultural differences to explore deeper values and ethical norms.

It is easy to see that the definition of ethics would be different between countries just as it is between companies. The biggest mistake companies make is assuming that *their* version of ethics matches everyone else's. This assumption can be very costly if not managed properly in advance like being suggested here.

- Create diverse, multinational teams to tackle global challenges. This ensures a variety of perspectives are considered in decision-making.
- Implement a global rotation program to give leaders firsthand experience in different cultural contexts. This immersion can provide invaluable insights into local ethical considerations.

This idea is like the cross-department tiger teams we discussed in the chapter on innovation in this book. Allowing your leaders to rotate will do more than any training class or seminar. We all know that experience is the best teacher.

- Encourage language learning among your leadership team to facilitate better communication and understanding across cultures.

Establish Global Ethical Standards
- Develop a global code of ethics that allows for cultural flexibility while maintaining core principles. This should be a collaborative process, involving input from all regions where you operate.
- Create local ethics committees in each major region to provide cultural context and guidance. These committees can help translate global principles into locally relevant practices.

- Regularly review and update your global ethics policies to ensure they remain relevant and effective. The global business landscape is constantly changing, and your ethical framework should evolve with it.
- Implement a system for sharing ethical best practices across regions, allowing for local innovations to benefit the entire organization.

Foster Global Dialogue
- Host annual global ethics summits bringing together leaders from all regions. Use these events to align on core principles and share regional perspectives.
- Implement a global ethical decision-making framework that considers cultural differences. This could include a step to specifically consider local cultural implications of decisions.
- Create a global ethics hotline that can handle reports in multiple languages, ensuring all employees have a way to raise concerns.
- Establish a global mentorship program pairing leaders from different cultural backgrounds to foster cross-cultural ethical understanding.

Unilever, under the leadership of Paul Polman, demonstrated how to lead ethically on a global scale. Their Sustainable Living Plan set ambitious targets for reducing environmental impact and improving social conditions across their global supply chain. Despite operating in over 190 countries, they maintained consistent ethical standards while allowing for local adaptation in implementation. Can you imagine that? 190 countries!

What Would a Wise Herd Leader Do?

Whenever I face a tough ethical decision, I like to think about the wise boss mares I have been describing in this book as well as some mentors like Coleman, my former CEO. These mares aren't always the biggest or the fastest, but they have an uncanny ability to make decisions that benefit the entire herd.

Shelby, the boss mare at Layla Rose Ranch, is the gentlest horse you will ever meet. She loves kids and is happy to let them love all over her. She is the mother of Layla, who is the ranch's namesake. I see her use her experience and instincts to make decisions that consider the long-term welfare of the entire group. She, like most boss mares, leads with integrity, not because they're forced to, but because it's ingrained in their nature.

As business leaders, we need to embody that same spirit. We need to lead with integrity, not because regulations demand it or because someone's watching, but because it's fundamental to who we are - it's part of our culture. We need to use our judgment, built from our experiences and values, to make decisions that benefit our entire "herd" - our employees, customers, stakeholders, and communities.

Like most reading this book, I have a ton of stories about unethical leaders I have worked with and sadly, fewer ethical ones. I am so thankful for the impact Coleman had on me when it comes to ethics.

When you're facing an ethical dilemma, ask yourself: "What would Shelby or Coleman do?" Would she take the easy path that only benefits a few, or would she face the challenge head-on, considering the needs of the entire herd?

Cultivating Ethical Leadership in Your Organization

Building a culture of ethical leadership isn't a one-time effort. It's an ongoing process that requires consistent attention and nurturing. A company's culture is a living, breathing part of your company. Every company has one whether they acknowledge it or not. In Chapter 3, we discussed the "Culture Cycle" which showed you how a culture develops.

In that discussion, you saw that your company's beliefs and values when it comes to ethics do not start from a poster or organizational document; they evolve from the programming of that culture which influences the beliefs and values and ultimately the behavior of the employees.

All through this chapter, I have tried to share some ideas with you to help "program" your culture to value ethics. Here are some strategies to help program ethical leadership into your organization's culture.

Develop Future Ethical Leaders

- Create a leadership development program that emphasizes ethical decision-making alongside other key skills.

Hopefully, you already have a strong leadership development program in your company but do an audit and see if it covers ethics. My experience is that very few companies ever overtly train on this topic. They may mention it or hang a poster about it. But most companies tend to believe that if you hire the right people, then ethics comes with it. Do you really believe that is true? Has that been your experience?

- Implement an ethical mentorship program, pairing experienced leaders with up-and-coming talent.

I learned this idea from a friend of mine who handles the mentor program at his company. They have a unique approach to mentorship. Rather than one person assigned to another, they assign based on topic. So, you may have a people development mentor and a financial mentor and, in this case, an ethics mentor.

He has found that by using multiple people it creates a well-rounded employee who gets to meet and learn from multiple leaders within the company. And ultimately, the training and mentorship is better since the expert on the topic is the one covering it. No matter how great any leader is, there are always areas that they are weaker in. My wife and former employees have all been kind enough to remind me of this.

- Encourage employees at all levels to take on ethical leadership roles, such as leading ethics discussions or spearheading corporate social responsibility initiatives.

Reward Ethical Behavior

- Make sure ethics are part of your recognition programs. This could be as simple as an "Ethical Leader of the Month" award or as significant as tying bonuses to ethical performance metrics.
- Share stories of ethical leadership throughout the organization. This not only recognizes those who've made tough ethical choices but also provides examples for others to follow.

On this idea, I would caution on calling it the "Ethical Story of the Month." Not sure anyone would want to read that. Plus, the key to ethics is to cover the principle and not the word. Meaning that if you are sharing a story that is related to good ethical behavior, it will have more impact than if you labeled it as such. Not that you need to be covert, but if you ask any employee if they are ethical, they all think they are. Remember, the number one reason employees don't do what they are supposed to is because they think they are!

- Consider ethical track records when making promotion decisions. Make it clear that climbing the corporate ladder requires more than just hitting financial targets.

Continuously Improve Your Ethical Framework

- Conduct regular ethical risk assessments to identify potential issues before they become problems.
- Solicit feedback from employees, customers, and other stakeholders on your organization's ethical performance.
- Stay informed about emerging ethical issues in your industry and be proactive in addressing them.
- Regularly update your code of ethics and ethical training programs to reflect new challenges and best practices.

This discussion on ethics certainly sounds like a lot. And you may be tempted to blow this chapter off under the header of "not that big of a problem for us." But just as soon as you do that, it can all go wrong. Your organization has the potential to navigate even the most challenging ethical terrain with grace and integrity if you plan in advance for that outcome.

As you move forward, consider these five questions:

1. How can you develop your ethical instincts to be more like Shelby's?
2. In what ways can you make ethical considerations for your entire "herd" a more integral part of your decision-making process?
3. How might you better foster a culture of trust and collective welfare in your organization, like the dynamics of a healthy horse herd?
4. What steps can you take to prepare your organization for ethical challenges in the global paddock, ensuring the welfare of your entire "herd"?
5. How can you inspire your team to lead with the wisdom and foresight of a trusted herd leader?

By wrestling with these questions and implementing some of the ideas from this chapter, you'll be well on your way to leading a more ethical, trustworthy, and successful organization. Like a herd of horses traversing both familiar pastures and unknown territories, your team will be equipped to navigate the complex global business landscape with integrity, reliability, and unwavering moral strength.

Remember, ethical leadership isn't just about avoiding wrongdoing - it's about actively doing what's right for the entire herd, even when it's difficult. By fostering a wise herd leader mentality in your leadership approach, you can unleash the full ethical potential of your organization and lead it to new heights of success and respect in the global paddock.

Chapter 9: Crisis Management and Resilience

In the unpredictable landscape of modern business, crisis management and resilience are crucial skills for any leader. Unfortunately, today, crisis seems to be a regular part of business life. Just as a horse herd must navigate through harsh weather, predator threats, and changing terrains, today's organizations face an ever-shifting array of challenges. By observing how horse herds handle crises and bounce back from adversity, we can glean some insights for leading our own "herds" through turbulent times.

Before we dive into practical strategies, let's take a moment to understand what crisis management and resilience really mean. Most of you reading probably deal with a lot of "crises" during your work week. And while little things pop up and employees make you crazy, the type of crisis we are discussing here is not you being a "fireman" putting out all the fires. It is deeper than that.

In a horse herd, where no email or Slack or chat exists, crisis management isn't just about reacting to immediate threats. It's a constant state of readiness, a collective vigilance that allows the herd to respond swiftly and effectively to any danger. The boss mare, much like an effective crisis manager, is always aware of her surroundings, ready to guide the herd to safety at a moment's notice.

Resilience, on the other hand, is the herd's ability to recover quickly from setbacks and adapt to new circumstances. It's not just about surviving a crisis, but about emerging stronger and more capable of facing future challenges.

At the Rescue, we see this resilience play out daily. The individual horse coming into the Rescue must show resilience to regain and rebuild trust. But the entire herd must demonstrate resilience in the fact that their world is an ever-changing life of new faces coming in and familiar faces leaving on a monthly basis.

When I think of effective crisis managers and resilient leaders, inspired by rescue horses of course, I think of these five key traits.

1. Be Vigilant: Always being aware of potential threats and opportunities.
2. Be Decisive: Making quick, informed decisions when time is of the essence.
3. Be Adaptable: Being able to change course rapidly in response to new information or circumstances.
4. Be Composed: Remaining calm under pressure to keep the entire herd from panicking.
5. Be a Good Communicator: Clearly conveying important information to the entire herd.

Let's use the rest of this chapter to unpack these in more detail to see how they can help your leadership.

1. Be Vigilant

As we mentioned before, with horses, preparation for a crisis isn't a separate activity - it's woven into the fabric of daily life. One might even say it is a cultural thing. Even while grazing peacefully, certain members of the herd remain alert, ready to sound the alarm at the first sign of danger. This constant state of readiness, without panic, is key to their survival.

I've observed this behavior countless times at our rescue ranch. Shelby and Cletus, our lead horses, are always checking on where everyone is in the pasture. It reminds me of how we, as parents, are always keeping an eye on our kids when they're out playing. The lead horse knows where the rest of the herd is by conducting regular check-ins. Sometimes this is a simple quick sound that the entire herd hears and understands immediately.

Here are some strategies to help your organization maintain this state of prepared vigilance. Remember, our goal is to give you a lot of ideas to choose from. You decide which ones make sense for your organization. You do not have to use all of them to be successful.

Develop Your Crisis Radar
- Implement regular risk assessments to identify potential threats to your organization.
- Create a crisis response team with clearly defined roles and responsibilities.
- Conduct "what-if" scenarios to prepare for various types of crises.

I know a CEO who loves this activity. One time after a P&L meeting - a meeting where our numbers were great, so we were all in a good mood - he said "congratulations everyone for a job well done. Now let's talk about disaster" Very motivational wouldn't you say?

He had us list possible "what if" scenarios and then we had to come up with some potential actions to deal with the scenarios if they did. The purpose was not to have all the answers in advance. The purpose was to get us to have a rhythm of being ready for when things do happen.

- Stay informed about industry trends and potential disruptors that could lead to crises.

Every effective CEO will tell you that an important part of his or her job is the macroeconomics of the business climate. Spend time reading about what is going on with the economy, market trends, consumer trends, etc. so that you can lead your team well. Think of it this way, we put so much on our department leaders that it is hard to expect them to tune into MSNBC or read the Wall Street Journal every day. That is part of your job as their leader.

Now, let me emphasize here that I am not talking about social media as your research tool. It is sad how much false information is posted every day. During the 2020 election, it was shown that nearly one out of every four posts on Facebook had false or misleading information. And I don't think it got any better in 2024. Even LinkedIn has been taken over by political opinion posts.

Practice Crisis Simulations
- Run regular crisis simulations to test your organization's readiness.
- Include different types of crises in your simulations, from natural disasters to PR nightmares.

I did an exercise with my team practicing potential PR nightmares after we had a real PR nightmare of our own. What I can tell you is that we handled the first one poorly for sure. But the next one, we were actually responsive versus reactive. And the effect on the company was significantly less.

We were practicing the "autopsy" approach. Debriefing and discussing what went right and what went wrong and the WHY for each. And as usual, the what went wrong part was a very long list. But we learned from it and improved. (I'll talk more about the autopsy a little later.)

Consider not only outward scenarios but also inward. I can recall some employee issues that we had to deal with that would have benefited from this approach. Always remember, anything you do in crisis mode sets precedent for how your company will think and respond.

- Evaluate and refine your crisis response plans based on these simulations.

- Involve employees at all levels in these exercises to build organization-wide crisis awareness.

Build a Culture of Preparedness
- Integrate crisis preparedness into your regular training programs.

Much like the discussion of ethics in a previous chapter, training programs rarely include this topic. And the best way to "program" your culture for crisis is to train on it in advance. When a crisis hits, time is not your friend. That time constraint causes us to make poor decisions, but if we are practicing and training in advance, then time is not as much of an enemy.

- Encourage employees to report potential risks or concerns without fear of retaliation.
- Regularly communicate the importance of crisis preparedness to all stakeholders.
- Recognize and reward vigilance and proactive risk management.

2. Be Decisive

I think this one is self-evident. However, when studying crisis management, this is where the most failures happen. Rather than making a decisive decision and driving forward, we tend to make little decisions that make us seem like we are responding to the crisis. When in reality, we are just delaying our response.

Make Decisive Decisions
- Gather necessary information quickly, but don't wait for perfect information before acting.
- Trust your instincts - they're often based on years of experience.
- Be willing to make tough calls when needed, always considering the welfare of the entire "herd".

Sorry that I keep going back to the pandemic for examples, but I think so many of us learned so much during that time. The one big lesson I took away from that time was the importance of making a decision. It was tough, wasn't it? Making decisions with so little data. None of us had led through that before. So, we were all learning.

Some of my contemporaries in other companies struggled to make decisions. I believe in the philosophy of "no decision before its time"- which as a principle is not a bad thing. But I don't think that it applies in crisis situations. They waited to make decisions on people and expense control and their people paid for it. I think the "great resignation" was partly driven by the inconsistency of companies or their indecisiveness during the pandemic. I am proud that we made decisions and owned them even if they did not work out the way we intended them too.

Show Empathy
- Acknowledge the emotional impact of the crisis on your team and stakeholders.
- Provide support resources for those affected by the crisis.
- Remember that your employees are people first - their wellbeing should be a top priority.

This one is big for leaders. Empathy is so important. Remember or equation for trust? Where compassion and confidence come together. The main ingredient in compassion for me is empathy.

The hardest task I ever face is having to layoff or terminate an employee. Even if the employee is at fault and the termination is just, the simple fact is that this man has to go home and tell his family he doesn't have a job.

I remember when it happened to me. As I shared with my three middle school aged girls what had happened, one of them asked "will we have to sell the house and move?" I keep that memory with me and try to be emphatic - no matter how upset I am with the employee - when communicating their status.

Focus on Solutions

- While acknowledging the reality of the situation, maintain a focus on finding solutions and moving forward.
- Encourage creative problem-solving from your team.
- Celebrate small wins and progress to maintain morale.

It is okay to be transparent during a crisis. You do not have all the answers. And that is okay. By nature, crisis is not something we prepare for is it? In fact, it is something we hope to never have to deal with. But always convey confidence in your decisions to balance your compassion.

3. Be Adaptable

Horse herds can recover quickly from setbacks, adapt to new environments, and continue to thrive in the face of ongoing challenges. This resilience is built into the very structure of the herd, with each member playing a role in the collective ability to bounce back.

However, it's important to note that this resilience isn't unlimited. At our Rescue, we often see horses that have been pushed beyond their limits by human mistreatment. These horses struggle to trust and integrate into new herds. The wounds are so deep that It can sometimes take several weeks or even months to get it back. Thankfully, my wife has that patience. It's a stark reminder that resilience must be nurtured and protected, not taken for granted.

Foster a Culture of Adaptability

- Encourage flexibility and willingness to change in response to new circumstances.
- Reward innovation and creative problem-solving.
- Provide training in adaptability and change management skills.

A culture develops through the "programming" it has placed into it. This programming can come from training, but more often than not, it comes from the behaviors of your employees. If you have a poster that says "Be Adaptable" on the wall, but none of your employees actually act that way, then it won't be a part of your culture. (Be honest, how many of you when you read the poster mentioned in the last sentence got the image of the kitten clinging from the tree limb with the words Hang in There at the top?)

Develop Redundancies

- Create backup systems and cross-train employees to ensure continuity in case of disruptions.
- Diversify your supply chain and customer base to reduce dependency on any single source.
- Maintain emergency funds or lines of credit to weather financial storms.

Encourage Continuous Learning

- Promote ongoing skill development to help your team adapt to new challenges.
- Create a culture where mistakes are seen as learning opportunities.
- Encourage knowledge sharing across departments and hierarchies.

If your company or team has to navigate a crisis, remember it is also a learning experience. So openly discuss what happened and what worked and what did not.

4. Be Composed

When a threat emerges, the boss mare in a horse herd demonstrates remarkable leadership. She remains calm, assesses the situation quickly, and guides the herd decisively. Her composure helps keep the entire herd from panicking, allowing for a coordinated response.

Interestingly, at our Rescue, I've noticed that the boss mare often "delegates" this responsibility to one of the males. Shelby, our lead mare, will often give a nod to Cletus, who then takes charge of gathering the herd when there's a perceived threat or potential danger. She even does this when it's not dangerous, but necessary. This collaborative approach ensures that the herd benefits from the strengths of multiple leaders.

I might note here that these threats happen more often than you think. As a prey animal horses are naturally programmed to believe that all things are a threat. There is a home not too far from our rescue with a dachshund named Pete. Pete likes to go wandering and oftentimes ends up on the ranch. I have pictures of the 5 lb. dachshund walking up to say hi to a 1200 lb. horse only to see that horse stop dead in its tracks and then run from the "horse-eating wiener dog."

Maintain Composure
- Practice stress management techniques to help you stay calm under pressure.
- Model the behavior you want to see in your team - if you panic, they will too.

- Develop a personal mantra or ritual to center yourself in times of crisis.

Shelby is amazingly calm. She is so good natured that we use her a lot at community events. She doesn't mind the kids touching all over her and is patient like no one else. The only time she shows emotion is when the other horses are not listening to her. Even when there is danger, she never really freaks out.

For example, in Texas we can get our share of severe thunderstorms. The thunder reverberates through the ranch and shakes the barn. When Shelby senses the storm, she will guide the others to the barn. She doesn't yell at them or chase them in a panic. In Shelby's mind there is no need to run. After all, a few raindrops never hurt anyone. (Although Cletus tends to run in. He is a bit of a diva.)

5. Be a Good Communicator

Many books have been written on the power of effective communication. And we will not try to create any new revelations here. But we do often overlook the tangential things of communication that matter as well. And during a crisis, they can be crippling.

Communicate Clearly and Frequently
- Establish clear communication channels for crisis situations.
- Provide regular updates to all stakeholders, even if the update is that there's no new information.
- Be transparent about what you know, what you don't know, and what you're doing to find out more.

I learned the importance of clear communication during the COVID-19 pandemic. At the company where I was CXO, we faced the not so unique challenge of having all our employees scattered and isolated. To address this, we instituted a weekly "state of the company" video sent to every employee every Friday. We focused on truth and transparency, even when the news wasn't good.

Like most companies, in order to survive 2020, we had to do layoffs. We decided to take all action in one move rather than dragging it out over several weeks. We felt this would release the tensions and worry. I know that many companies did several small RIFs because they did not want to cut people if ultimately they would not have too. But this practice kept the entire company in a constant state of consternation. And the casualty was work performance and productivity.

In our weekly videos, we explained what was happening that week including when we did the layoffs and what it meant for the future. Many employees told us that these weekly updates made all the difference during that uncertain time.

We told the truth in every video. I think many companies would be trying to "spin" the information in an effort to reduce panic, but we did not. We knew the chances of someone leaving were real, but we chose to communicate clearly, with raw authenticity and with the calm mentioned earlier.

I think it's important for employees to know that their leaders know they are fallible. Your learning should include examples of when it was done wrong and not just done right. Unfortunately, I have too many stories in my life about broken bones, but never from diving in front of a speeding car to save a small child. More like, getting injured when my dad wanted to move the washing machine with our wheelbarrow and my job was to "steady" it from the front. You know how that ended. I got some serious learning - and a cast.

Build Strong Networks
- Develop robust relationships with suppliers, partners, and customers to create a support system.
- Foster a sense of community within your organization.
- Engage with industry peers to share best practices and support each other during crises.

This is one of those tangential areas I was referring too. We practiced the same transparency with our suppliers during COVID that we did with our employees.
We talked to each other and "shared" our thoughts as partners. We did not apply a one solution fits all approach to our vendors and their bills.

We spoke to each and asked them what success looked like during that time. Honestly, I was surprised there were different answers from the various vendors. If you had asked me in advance, I would have bet they all wanted the same thing. But they didn't. We emerged with stronger vendor relationships because of it.

Promote Well-being
- Support the physical and mental health of your team to build individual and collective resilience.
- Implement stress management programs and provide mental health resources.
- Encourage work-life balance to prevent burnout.

One of the things we did during the pandemic was to have virtual happy hours. We got this idea from another company, so sorry that we stole the idea, but it really helped us during a tough time.

As we all know, everyone who was stuck at home, trying to do their job, was stressed out. I was stir crazy after a few hours. (If you recall, that is how the horse rescue got started in the first place.) If everyone was stressed about what was happening in their world, our task became a focus on how we can keep all of our employees healthy and "in the game" while being stuck remote - especially those, like me, who were used to working in an office with other humans all day.

The virtual happy hours were held via Zoom. We played games like Two Truths and a Lie and focused on making our employees smile. No work talk. Just fun. And they were fun. Especially when we got to see everyone's home environment.

Learning from Crisis: The Herd's Collective Memory

After facing a threat, horses don't simply return to normal. They integrate the experience into their collective knowledge, adjusting their behaviors and remaining more alert to similar dangers in the future. This ability to learn and adapt from each challenge enhances their long-term resilience. Think of Shelby sensing the storm. The more times she dealt with this, the more adept she became leading when the storm approached.

In the business world, we saw this adaptive learning play out during and after the COVID-19 pandemic didn't we? Many organizations, including my own, discovered that remote work could be effective and even beneficial in some cases. We adapted to a new hybrid model, allowing employees to work from home one or two days a week. This change, born out of necessity during a crisis, has become a new norm that benefits both the company and its employees.

Here are some ideas to help your organization learn effectively from crises. (By the way, I hope you don't have any crises.)

Conduct a Thorough Review

- Analyze what worked well and what could be improved in your crisis response.
- Involve all levels of the organization in this review process.
- Document lessons learned and integrate them into your crisis management plans.

At my last company, we called this process an "autopsy." After any significant event or project, we would gather all stakeholders to debrief what worked and what didn't. We would capture these learnings in writing, always looking for opportunities to apply them in our daily operations.

Our CEO, a former F-16 pilot named Coleman, would set the stage for these meetings by telling everyone we were going to practice "Blameless Problem Solving." This approach, borrowed from his military experience, helped keep everyone focused on improvement rather than finger-pointing.

We conducted these autopsies, not just when things went poorly, but as part of our culture. We followed a Four-Part cycle in all company efforts:

Plan - Brief - Execute - Debrief

Debrief, obviously, is the autopsy. To help guide this debrief, Coleman used the acronym STEALTH. I'm not sure if it was his original thought or he got it from the Air Force, but either way, I'm grateful.

STEALTH stood for:

Set the Time
Tone - Blameless
Execution - Did we meet the Objective?
Analyze - the root causes of success or failure
Lessons Learned
Transfer Knowledge - He made us write it out
High Note - he always wanted us to end on a high note, no matter how bad the autopsy revealed us to be.

You will see this model reflected in this entire section. I lived through it many times and it was a terrific tool. If nothing else in this book, that model makes it worth the donation to the Rescue.

Share Learnings

- Communicate insights gained from the crisis throughout the organization.
- Create case studies based on your crisis experience to use in future training.
- Share your learnings with industry peers to contribute to collective resilience.

Today's worker wants more than a paycheck from their job; they want to be part of something. They want their job to have purpose and meaning and they want to know that the people they work for are honest and transparent.

There is no better way to do this than by sharing your learnings. I attended some virtual networking events that focused on key learnings from the pandemic year. I was relieved to hear similar plans like ours. And I was challenged by some even better ideas I wished I would have thought of. But it was all part of sharing our learnings on a larger scale outside of the company.

Recognize Contributions

- Acknowledge individuals and teams who played key roles in managing the crisis.
- Use crisis response as a way to identify emerging leaders in your organization.
- Celebrate the resilience and adaptability of your team.

I have tried to recognize Coleman for his role in teaching me some solid crisis management tools in this chapter. It is my way to recognize his contribution to my career. Make sure you take time to tell the stories and celebrate the heroes of your company after the dust settles.

Integrate New Practices

- Identify positive changes or innovations that emerged during the crisis and integrate them into regular operations.
- Be open to reimagining "business as usual" based on crisis learnings.
- Update your crisis management plans, and business continuity strategies based on real-world experience.

Here is where most companies stop. They manage the crisis. They hold a Debrief or autopsy to discuss it. But they take no time to document it and create a process for next time.

I get the tension. We just spent all our time and mental and emotional strain on a crisis. And what we want most now is to have it all behind us. Plus, we are way behind on our normal work, so the tendency to stop short of this last step is all too tempting.

Crisis Management Across Cultures

Just as different horse herds might have slightly different social norms, different cultures have varying approaches to crisis management. Navigating this global landscape requires sensitivity, adaptability, and a strong ethical core. Hopefully, we established this in the last chapter.

With the Rescue, my wife doesn't focus on the breed, she focuses on the need. Which means we have had horses from many breeds - from Tennessee Walkers (her favorite) to Mustangs to Thoroughbreds to Arabians to Drafts. Think of each of these breeds like their own country. Each breed has its own social norms and standards and when it gets integrated into a mixed herd like we have at the Rescue, you can see the dynamics of the horses trying to navigate the herd.

After quarantine and passing medical clearance with the vet, it is time for the horse to be brought into the herd. But my wife never lets the horse directly in. She puts the new rescue into a pasture or paddock that shares a fence with the other horses. They spend the first week getting to know each other over the fence. Since sometimes the breed differences can be dramatic, she is trying to avoid unnecessary physical confrontation between the horses.

Eventually, she will place them all together. And the horses still have some work to do. They struggle a bit integrating and assimilating, but because of her introductory approach, the new rescue gets to observe the patterns and behaviors of the herd before joining. So, it is not a complete shock. The horse knows what to expect and what it needs to adapt going into the herd.

Here are some strategies for effective crisis management in a global context. These ideas are from interviewing and studying people much smarter than me in this area. And they were gracious enough to help me craft some ideas for your team.

Develop Cultural Intelligence
- Provide cross-cultural training for all employees, especially those in leadership positions.
- Create diverse, multinational teams to tackle global challenges.
- Implement a global rotation program to give leaders firsthand experience in different cultural contexts.

Establish Global Crisis Management Standards
- Develop a global crisis management framework that allows for cultural flexibility while maintaining core principles.
- Create local crisis response teams in each major region to provide cultural context and on-the-ground response.
- Regularly review and update your global crisis management policies to ensure they remain relevant and effective.

Foster Global Dialogue
- Host annual global crisis management summits bringing together leaders from all regions.
- Implement a global crisis communication system that can handle multi-lingual, multi-cultural communication.
- Establish a global mentorship program pairing leaders from different cultural backgrounds to foster cross-cultural understanding in crisis situations.

One expert that I interviewed really pushed the idea of mentorship. She shared that if we leave the training to PowerPoint or Google Slides, we are missing the subtle nuances of cultures that tend to be the "land mine" hidden beneath the surface that is unintentionally and inadvertently stepped on.

"When people share in a mentor setting, they can express the subtleties that get lost in training decks," she explained. How you say something is as important as what you say.

<u>Cultivating Crisis Management Skills in Your Organization</u>

Building a culture of effective crisis management and resilience isn't a one-time effort. It's an ongoing process that requires consistent attention and nurturing. Here are some strategies to help embed crisis management skills into your organization's culture:

Develop Future Crisis Leaders
- Create a leadership development program that emphasizes crisis management skills alongside other key competencies.
- Implement a crisis management mentorship program, pairing experienced leaders with up-and-coming talent.
- Encourage employees at all levels to participate in crisis simulations and planning exercises.

Reward Crisis Management Skills
- Create recognition programs that highlight effective crisis management.
- Share stories of successful crisis navigation throughout the organization.
- Consider crisis management track records when making promotion decisions.

Continuously Improve Your Crisis Management Framework
- Conduct regular crisis management audits to identify potential weaknesses in your system.
- Solicit feedback from employees, customers, and other stakeholders on your organization's crisis response capabilities.

- Stay informed about emerging crisis management best practices and be proactive in adopting them.

By embracing the resilient spirit of a wise herd leader, you can create an environment where effective crisis management becomes second nature. Remember, like a well-functioning horse herd, your organization has the potential to navigate even the most challenging crises with grace and resilience.

As you move forward, consider these five questions:

1. How can you develop your crisis management instincts to be more like Shelby's ability to remain calm and decisive in the face of danger?
2. In what ways can you make crisis preparedness a more integral part of your organization's daily operations?
3. How might you better foster a culture of resilience in your organization, like the collective strength of a healthy horse herd?
4. What steps can you take to prepare your organization for crises in the global landscape, ensuring the welfare of your entire "herd"?
5. How can you inspire your team to lead with the wisdom and foresight of a trusted herd leader during times of crisis?

By wrestling with these questions and implementing some of the ideas from this chapter, you'll be well on your way to leading a more resilient, prepared, and successful organization.

Effective crisis management isn't just about surviving challenges - it's about emerging stronger and more capable. I feel like the company that emerged after the pandemic that I was leading was just that - stronger - and it showed in our performance in the months following the pandemic. I was proud to be part of a team that handled crisis so well. Fostering this mentality in your approach to crises, you can unleash the full resilient potential of your organization and lead it to new heights of success and respect in the global business world.

Chapter 10: Embracing the Lessons from the Herd - Your Leadership Journey

As we reach the final stretch of our journey through the world of rescue horse-inspired leadership, I want you to take a moment to reflect. Close your eyes and imagine yourself standing at the edge of a vast, sun-dappled meadow. The air is crisp and clean, filled with the gentle sounds of a horse herd grazing peacefully nearby. What do you see as you observe this herd?

You see strength in unity as the horses move together across the landscape, their movements synchronized in a beautiful dance of cooperation. You notice clear, purposeful communication in every flick of an ear, every shift of posture. You witness resilience as the herd navigates challenges, adapting seamlessly to changes in their environment. Most strikingly, you observe a perfect balance between individual needs and collective wellbeing. But beyond all of this, you see something even more profound - a reflection of your own potential as a leader.

Throughout this book, we've explored how the wisdom of rescue horses can transform your leadership approach. We've delved into the intricate dynamics of horse herds and drawn parallels to your world of organizational leadership. Now, as we conclude our journey, it's time to challenge yourself to put these lessons into practice. Are you ready to lead with the wisdom of the herd?

Let's revisit some of the key concepts we've explored and consider how you can apply them in your leadership journey.

Remember our discussion on herd mentality and understanding herd leadership? We talked about Shelby, our boss mare, and how her leadership style embodied qualities that every great leader should aspire to. Her quiet authority, clear communication, and decisive action always considered the welfare of the entire herd. How can you embody these qualities in your daily leadership?

Challenge yourself to lead with calm assurance rather than reactivity. When faced with a difficult situation tomorrow, ask yourself: "**What would Shelby do?**" Would she panic and create chaos, or would she assess the situation calmly and guide her herd with confidence? Try to embody that calm, assured presence in your own leadership style.

Recall our exploration of building your leadership corral. We discussed how a skilled horse trainer like my wife creates a safe space for learning and growth, establishing clear boundaries and fostering trust. How can you create a similar environment for your team? Consider the boundaries you've set in your organization. Are they clear? Are they consistent? Do they provide the right balance of structure and freedom that allows your team to thrive?

Challenge yourself to be more consistent in your communication and actions. Remember, just like horses in a herd, your team is always watching you, picking up on subtle cues about what's acceptable and what's not. Your actions speak louder than your words, so ensure they're aligned.

We delved deep into the importance of corporate culture, likening it to the unwritten rules that govern a horse herd. Think of your company's culture as a living, breathing entity - because it is. Every action you take, every decision you make, is shaping this culture. What story is your leadership telling? Is it one of trust, innovation, and collective success? Or is it inadvertently rewarding behaviors that don't align with your vision?

Take a moment to reflect on the culture you're creating. Are you fostering an environment where people feel safe to take risks and innovate? Are you promoting collaboration over competition? Are you recognizing and rewarding the behaviors that align with your organization's values? Be intentional about the culture you're creating. Remember, **culture isn't formed by what you say, but by what you do** consistently over time.

Communication emerged as a central theme in our journey. We marveled at how horses communicate volumes without uttering a single word. How can you refine your non-verbal communication to be as clear and effective? **Challenge yourself to listen more deeply**, to pick up on the subtle cues your team is constantly sending. Are you truly hearing what isn't being said?

Practice being more present in your interactions. Put away distractions and give your full attention to the person you're communicating with. Watch for non-verbal cues, listen for the emotion behind the words. Like a horse attuned to the slightest shift in its environment, train yourself to pick up on the nuances of human communication.

Remember our discussion on the art of training? We drew parallels between horse training and people development, highlighting the importance of preparing the learner, setting the stage, establishing authority, and using the "pressure and release" technique. How can you incorporate these ideas into your people development strategies?

Consider how you're approaching training and development in your organization. Are you preparing your team members adequately before asking them to take on new challenges? Are you setting the stage for learning by creating an environment where it's safe to make mistakes? Are you establishing your authority through trust and respect rather than fear or coercion? And are you using the "pressure and release" technique - applying pressure to encourage growth, then releasing to allow integration of learning?

Remember, true **learning is a change in behavior,** not just knowledge acquisition. How can you ensure that the training you provide translates into real, observable changes in how your team operates?

We uncovered the powerful truth that all behavior is rewarded, even if unintentionally. This principle is crucial in shaping your organization. Take a hard look at what behaviors you're actually reinforcing. Are they aligned with your goals and values? Don't be afraid to make changes if they're not.

For instance, are you inadvertently rewarding crisis management by always praising the person who puts out fires, while overlooking the quiet efficiency of those who prevent crises from happening in the first place? Are you reinforcing a culture of overwork by consistently recognizing those who work long hours, rather than those who work smarter? **Challenge yourself to be more intentional about what you reward and recognize**.

Innovation was another key theme, inspired by the free-spirited nature of wild horses. How can you create an environment where creativity flourishes? Challenge yourself to foster a culture where ideas can run free, yet still work together towards a common goal, just like a herd of wild horses.

Consider implementing regular brainstorming sessions where all ideas are welcome. Create safe spaces for experimentation and failure. Remember, not every innovation will succeed, but **without the freedom to try new things, groundbreaking ideas will never have the chance to emerge**.

Ethical leadership in our global "paddock" reminded us of the importance of integrity. Like a trusted herd leader, are you making decisions based on what's best for the entire group, even when it's challenging? Your team is looking to you for moral guidance. Be the leader they can trust to do the right thing, even when no one is watching.

Challenge yourself to be more transparent in your decision-making processes. When faced with ethical dilemmas, involve your team in discussions about the right course of action. Not only will this help in making more balanced decisions, but it will also model ethical thinking for your entire organization.

Finally, recall our exploration of crisis management and resilience. Horse herds face threats with vigilance, decisiveness, adaptability, composure, and clear communication. How can you embody these qualities in your leadership, especially during challenging times?

Practice scenario planning with your team. What potential crises could your organization face? How would you respond? By thinking through these scenarios in advance, you'll be better prepared to face real challenges when they arise. Remember, **resilience isn't just about surviving - it's about emerging stronger and more capable**.

<u>Transformation Starts Today</u>

Transforming your leadership style is a journey, not a destination. Like working with rescue horses, it requires patience, consistency, and a willingness to learn and adapt. There will be challenges along the way, moments where you might stumble or doubt yourself. But remember the resilience of those rescue horses - how they overcome their past traumas to become strong, trusting partners. **You too have that strength within you**.

Think about Cletus, our cover star. When he was first rescued, he was mistrustful and defensive. But with patience, consistency, and compassionate leadership, he transformed into a confident, reliable partner. Your leadership journey may have similar ups and downs. There may be times when you feel like you're not making progress, or when old habits creep back in. In these moments, channel Cletus's resilience. Remember that growth isn't always linear, but with persistence and the right mindset, **transformation is always possible**.

As you move forward, keep the wisdom of the herd close to your heart. Lead with presence, authenticity, and a deep connection to those you lead. Foster unity while honoring individual strengths. Communicate with clarity and purpose. Adapt to changing circumstances with grace and resilience. Make decisions that benefit the entire "herd."

Consider starting a leadership journal. Each day, write down one way you applied a lesson from this book in your leadership practice. Reflect on what worked well and what you might do differently next time. This practice of reflection and continuous improvement is key to growing as a leader.

Most importantly, never stop learning and growing. Stay curious, stay humble, and stay open to the lessons that surround you every day. The moment you think you know everything is the moment you stop growing as a leader. Like a horse always alert to its environment, keep your senses attuned to new ideas, perspectives, and opportunities for growth.

Remember, you're not just leading a team - you're guiding a herd. Your actions have the power to inspire, to transform, to create a legacy of positive change. Embrace this responsibility with courage and compassion. Every interaction, every decision, is an opportunity to model the kind of leadership that can change not just your organization, but the world.

Let's end with some thoughts for your personal leadership journey.

Your Daily Leadership Practice

Transforming your leadership style doesn't happen overnight. It requires consistent, mindful practice. Here are some ways to incorporate horse-inspired leadership into your daily routine:

- **Morning Reflection**: Start each day by embodying the calm, alert presence of a lead mare. Take a few minutes to center yourself and set your intentions for the day.
- **Communication Check**: Before each interaction, pause and consider how you can communicate with the clarity and purpose of a herd leader.

- **Unity Booster**: Look for one opportunity each day to foster unity within your team, inspired by the cohesiveness of a horse herd.
- **Adaptability Challenge**: Intentionally seek out one situation daily where you can practice flexibility and innovative thinking.
- **Ethical Compass Check**: At the end of each day, reflect on your decisions. Did they align with the principle of leading for the good of the entire "herd"?

Your Leadership Learning Plan

Continuous learning is a cornerstone of horse-inspired leadership. Develop a personal learning plan to deepen your understanding and skills:

- **Read Widely**: Commit to reading one leadership book per month, including titles outside your usual scope.
- **Seek Mentorship**: Identify a leader you admire who embodies horse-inspired principles. Approach them for mentorship.
- **Experiential Learning**: Look for opportunities to observe horse herds in person. What new insights can you gain?
- **Teach Others**: Share your learning journey with your team. Teaching others will deepen your own understanding.
- **Reflect and Journal**: Keep a leadership journal. Regular reflection will help you internalize and apply what you're learning.

Visualize the leader you want to become:

- How do you want your team to perceive you?
- What impact do you want to have on your organization?
- How will you embody the wisdom of the herd in your daily actions?

Hold this vision in your mind as you move forward. Let it guide your decisions and actions.

Finally, as you step away from this book and back into your own leadership arena, rather than five questions, let me give you five thoughts to carry with you:

Trust Your Instincts: Like horses, we humans have an innate wisdom that often speaks to us in quiet ways. Learn to listen to and trust your instincts. They are the accumulation of your experiences and insights, much like the collective wisdom of the herd.

Embrace Your Unique Leadership Style: Just as each horse in the herd has its own personality and strengths, your leadership style is uniquely yours. Embrace it. Refine it. Let it be shaped by the wisdom of the herd but always remain authentically you.

Lead with Heart: At its core, horse-inspired leadership is about connection - to your team, to your purpose, to the larger ecosystem in which you operate. Lead not just with your head, but with your heart.

Never Stop Learning: The herd is always alert, always adapting. Make a commitment to lifelong learning. The moment you think you know everything is the moment you stop growing as a leader.

Pass It On: As you grow in your horse-inspired leadership journey, become a mentor to others. Share your insights, your struggles, your triumphs. Help cultivate the next generation of leaders who will carry this wisdom forward.

My Prayer for You

May your leadership journey be as free-spirited as Cheyenne our wild mustang, always ready to explore new frontiers. May it be as strong and reliable as Cletus, our steadfast gelding, providing a solid foundation for your team to rely on. And may it be as wise and nurturing as Shelby, our seasoned boss mare, always considering the wellbeing of the entire herd in every decision.

The paddock of possibility lies before you – vast, exciting, and full of potential. You have within you the wisdom of the herd, the lessons of the rescue horses, and your own unique strengths as a leader. Trust in these, lean on them, let them guide you as you guide others.

Lead on, with the grace, strength, and intuition inspired by our rescue horse teachers. The world is waiting for the leader you're becoming. Your herd is ready to follow you to new heights of success, innovation, and positive impact. The journey ahead may be challenging at times, but it's also filled with incredible opportunities for growth, both for you and for those you lead.

Remember, every great journey begins with a single step. So, take that step now. Apply one lesson from this book today. Then another tomorrow. Day by day, step by step, you'll be creating a new model of leadership – one inspired by the timeless wisdom of rescue horses, but uniquely your own.

Go forth and lead your herd to greatness. The meadow is yours to explore, the path is yours to forge. Lead with courage, with compassion, and with the unshakeable bond of the herd always in your heart. Your leadership journey starts now – make it extraordinary.

About the Author - Matthew Hudson

Matthew Hudson has been blessed with a varied career leading in companies of all sizes. He has a PhD in Organizational Behavior and is a sought-after speaker with a gift for bringing light to the complex. He is president of Layla Rose Ranch Horse Rescue and is married to its founder Catherine. He is available for consulting and speaking engagements.
matt@hudsonhead.com

About the Rescue - Layla Rose Ranch

Started in 2000 with her first rescue, Cletus (the one on the cover of this book), Catherine Hudson founded Layla Rose Ranch, an 11-acre dedicated facility for the rescue of abused, neglected and forgotten horses given up for slaughter.

Layla Rose Ranch follows a 3-step process.
Rescue - from a life of hopelessness
Restore - trust in humans and themselves
Relive - the life they were created to live in a forever home

To find our more or donate to help go to laylaroseranch.org

Scan to donate!

Order other books by Matt on Amazon.com

Culturrific!
Creating an experiential culture in your
organization.
$19.95

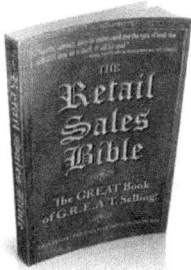

The Retail Sales Bible
The G.R.E.A.T. Selling System for Retail. Written for
retail sales professionals.
$19.95

Advisor Selling
The art and science of becoming a trusted sales
advisor. Written for B2B sales reps.
$19.95

Signs Sell
Harnessing the Power of Your Interior
Advertising
$25.95

www.ingramcontent.com/pod-product-compliance
Lightning Source LLC
Chambersburg PA
CBHW060611210326
41519CB00014B/3629